To Reverend John C. Dorr Jr.
and all the folks of
Peachtree Corners Associate Reformed Presbyterian Church

Table of Contents

Introduction 9
   Stewart Shipp's Stewardship Commitment 9
   The Four Basics of Christian Stewardship 18

Chapter One: Worship 19
   A Personalized Worship Service 21
   So We Give… 23
   Church Books Reveal That Offerings Are Not Needed .. 25
   What's All the Cheering About? 27
   Setting Up a Trust Program 29
   Letter to Stewart Shipp 31
   How Rich and Wise Were Those Rich Wise Men? 34
   A Resolution for the Tender-Hearted 37

Chapter Two: Service 41
   Stewardship Time-Machine Discovered 43

- Of Katrina and Things and Time and Stewardship........46
- Don't Give Those Jokers Another Dime........................48
- Christmas with Mr. Potato Head....................................51
- Stewart Shipp Is Off For The Summer 53

Chapter Three: Tithing 55
- Investment Prophet Extols Tithing Profit 57
- Be All That You Were Meant To Be 59
- A Plan To Pray Like We Give 62
- I See They're Playing Golf.
  Can This Really Be Heaven? 65
- O Lord! What Have You Done with
  the Amway Guy?...68
- Tithing By the Numbers for *Dummies*...........................71

Chapter Four: Prosperity 79
- God's Prosperity Promises Are About Him, Not You.....81
- Everybody Has a Buddy 90
- Giving Thanks First...93
- Ten Million Dollars Pledged to Local Church 96
- Practical Stewart Shipp Advice
  with A Divine Return...99

About the Authors...103
- Stewart R. Shipp: The Real Skinny...............................103
- Stewart R. Shipp and Me 105

Introduction

Stewart Shipp's Stewardship Commitment

I go by the name Stewart R. Shipp. I write a monthly column for the *Chimes*. A lot of times when I tell people that I write for the *Chimes,* they jump to the conclusion that I write for the *Times,* or at least the *China Times.* Nope, I write for the *Chimes.* For the past couple of years or so, I have written a monthly article about giving and stewardship practices for my church, Peachtree Corners Associate Reformed Presbyterian Church. The *Chimes* refers to the bell steeple on our church building. The chimes ring every hour during the day. Actually, there's no bell—just a recording that plays *Westminster Chimes* and then gongs the number of the hour. It doesn't play at noon on Sunday, because that might interrupt Pastor Dorr if his sermon runs too long. The Church Elders directed the Deacons to turn off the Chimes every Sunday at noon. (The Deacons did, but they put up a clock in the back of the church for Pastor Dorr to see.) For a lot of churches today, messages about Christian stewardship have been turned off and considered to be "turn-offs." It's time to sound the chimes again for the Christian discipline of stewardship. That's my commitment. That's been my assignment.

Often the journalist's beat is a grind. Even more often, any mention of Christian stewardship is a grind. I'll have to say that for me, my assignment has been fun. More than that, it has been fulfilling. Honestly, it has been helpful in my stewardship journey through my personal Christian experience. Each article is rather short. *Chimes* column space is dear and editorial allocation is competitive. Many times the editors were grateful for the content to fill up one of the eight pages of information about the usual goings-on at our church. Every now and then my monthly article was bumped, because the church had so many more things going here in Peachtree Corners. Stewardship messages are susceptible to such.

I've often heard that these brief articles are not only amusing, but bring understanding to others. The understanding part was my primary objective. So, I thought that it might be a good idea to compile these messages into a book. You are holding the results of that idea. I hope that my intentions of helping you to understand my interpretations of Christian stewardship succeed. If they amuse you, so much the better.

NOTE: At anytime, you're welcome to skip on over to those articles. You opened this book for your own reasons, which probably is not another homily on stewardship. I would like for you to come back to this introduction for my ideas about stewardship. I'd like a chance to explain my reason for writing this book. Now come on back—I'll be right here.

Introduction

You might assume that I was born with a generous heart for the Christian stewardship ministry. You'd be wrong though. Furthermore, I'm not sure that I had any childhood instructions on giving. I know that my dad frequently put an envelope in the church offering, but I have no idea what the contents were. Frankly, my passion has grown gradually, very gradually over so many, many years. I pray that it will continue to grow, but I pray that I can lead you to a fuller understanding of the power and joy of Christian stewardship. Many of my Christian family of friends have reaped the true fruits of abiding in God's word. The most recognizable fruits are my friends' peaceful resilience in situations which normally would be unsettling financial short falls. I seek such resilience. I seek such joy. Many times I've found it. I want it more often. I want it all the time. I pray that you may have the same, too.

It would be great if more folks today shared the joy of Christian stewardship. Obviously, we of this era are not the first generation with financial stress. Even in Biblical times the people were burdened and anxious with accumulating debt, stretching for paydays, and sudden financial losses. Jesus himself was a carpenter, Paul was a tent-maker, and Peter was a fisherman. They could be described as businessmen. I have always assumed that they were sole proprietors in their operations. Maybe Peter had formed a partnership with his brother, Andrew. Paul was evidently a contract tentmaker during his missionary journeys. I'll bet he owned his own place, though, when he was a Pharisee. Jesus worked for his dad. I've done that, so as a boss's son I love Jesus even the more. Surely they were confronted with the financial woes that we also endure in the 21st century. In their careers they were more than likely stiffed by a few non-paying customers. Occasionally, a vendor must have failed to deliver materials on time. Their investment decisions may have been no greater than buying a new drop-net or a crosscut saw, but they had the same return on investment uncertainties that present day business managers confront. Perhaps the difference is a matter of degree or the addition of a few zeroes on now-inflated currency, but their financial worries were obviously stressful.

I know this is true; otherwise, Jesus wouldn't have spent so much of His ministry talking about money, finances and stewardship. I've heard that 30% of His parables deal with money. (Someday I'll audit that number.) In a simple age with a simple economic structure, His followers were anxious about their financial future, worried about the security of their loved ones, and unsure about their own abilities to make it through the storms. In many of Jesus' parables we can see the anxiety about money, financial security, and wealth accumulation.

I don't want to minimize the stress that the Biblical characters carried, but I don't believe that today's financial environment could be imaginable in Biblical times. Shekels, denari, talents, and silver coins meant a lot to Biblical businessmen; such coinage meant a day's, or a week's, or a year's wages. Decisions affecting wages are pressure-packed, for sure. Yet, today, even junior bank officials are responsible for millions of dollars—enough to be the annual wages for an entire town. We're clearly not in Biblical times today. So, if today's Christians are in such need for stewardship training and if Jesus spent so much effort teaching His disciples about finances, why do today's preachers spend so little pulpit time on stewardship—especially financial stewardship?

Simple Biblical Times : Substantial Stewardship Teachings

Complex Times Today : Limited Stewardship Teachings

Today, more than ever, we need to understand good, strong stewardship principles. Intuitively, I think we know the common answers for this paucity of stewardship teaching.

The Visiting Rich Young Ruler

First of all, few preachers like to talk about money. Well, that's not true. Some TV preachers make a career out of talking about nothing but money. But for the most part the local pastor is reluctant to preach about money. On the other hand, every preacher would like his pastorate to have more money for church purposes. An easy solution to this paradox is for the church to have an individual benefactor who can support the "extra" things that come up, and who will do so without too much groveling by the preacher. Not all churches have such a benefactor. That potential benefactor may show up on any Sunday. What preacher doesn't fear that if a stewardship message is planned, the rich man like in the Gospels, his church's future benefactor, might show up as a first time visitor only to be turned off by a money-talk sermon. Or, equally as daunting, if there is already an in-house benefactor, he has let it be known that money-talk is taken personally and is out of place in the sermon. As much as a benefactor is desired, we don't want to look like we have an eye for their pocketbooks…even though we may.

Apparently, seminaries teach a certain reverence toward rich folks. Bolstered by the church treasurer, it is common for the preacher to eschew the wonderful messages of Christian stewardship as inapplicable to rich folks. If they are rich, then they must be smart. If they are smart, then they must know enough about money management. They don't need any more guidance. It's difficult to see any good coming from a poorly timed stewardship message, if the rich visitor "…went away sad, because he had great wealth" (Matt. 10:22).[1] However, those rich visitors may be the very ones most in need of these messages. Never mind the high probability that most may be fretful about preserving their fortunes tied up in secular financial traps

---

[1] All scripture references cited are from Zondervan New International Version.

or unable to focus on anything else going on around them. For good or bad, they are stewards of more resources than the rest of the congregation put together. They are the perfect audience for Christian stewardship messages. We should hope that at the next stewardship sermon, several rich visitors would show up. It might be good for them.

Don't lay the entire burden on preachers, though. How often in our evangelistic outreach do we recruit the affluent, the sophisticated, and the popular? It seems that we honor the wealthy—even those made wealthy solely by secular circumstances. We should look at all souls in anticipation of what Jesus Christ will make of them. I'm sure that's the way Christ desires our outreach. But that's a topic for someone else's book.

The Money-Grabber Tag Line

A preacher doesn't want to give the idea that his Christian church is just another organization trying to get your membership first, then ultimately your pocketbook. I've prepared business strategy models for many companies, but I'm not sure this misguided idea holds water. If profitability were the objective of teaching stewardship, the concept goes something like this: The Christian Church is an organization that believes in God. The Church follows Gods' word. God created the whole world. God is the sovereign ruler of the whole world. God suffered death on the cross for this world. God led Paul and other saints to build the Church. God revealed certain instructions to have church members give some portion of their income and wealth to Him—both as worship and for service. From the largess of these members, He would then be able to "grab money" from His churches. With that money He can acquire things for Himself. Yet, He made all these things in the first place. So, as a sovereign creator He carries out a plan that includes the death of His only Son, in order to have what he already has. That's not a particularly logical business model. Like it or not, our local church may be seen to be a money-grabbing organization. So why tempt fate? To be safe, the pragmatic pastor just avoids the sermons about Christian stewardship.

Prosperity Doctrine Phobia

If a preacher spends too much time on financial talk, he might be seen as no better than those TV evangelists constantly whining about nothing but their waning cash balances. Preaching on everyday financial issues may cause the un-churched to view the local church as promoting "works" theology, so that they miss the good news of God's grace. Consequently, the common lore is that until the congregation has reached a certain Christian maturity level, the deep meaning of Christian stewardship should be withheld until each new Christian is firmly grounded in the other Christian disciplines. This rationale is that God promises prosperity through the discipline of giving. TV hucksters recite these promises, perhaps with great distortion, then receive gazillions of dollars from the hopelessly hopeful audience and succumb to tawdry lifestyles far from the Christian path. Therefore, God's promises must be carefully interpreted, because TV hucksters so easily abuse them.

The message, then, to our local pastors is, "Don't mention God's promises of prosperity, because they can so easily be misinterpreted, if not abused." Until the congregation as a whole has reached a certain level of understanding, stay away from the prosperity messages. There's plenty of other material in the Bible to preach about. Be aware that there is no known indication as to when a congregation has reached that mysterious level of understanding and is ready for stewardship sermons.

Traditional Stewardship Season Timing

Most every church has its own long tradition that has become sacrosanct. Any change in "the way we've always done it" is considered close to heresy. For Christian stewardship, that holy-of-holies is the reverent observance of the stewardship season. There is no clear definition of exactly when stewardship season actually is. Each congregation is different, but there are certain ironclad dictums for most of them that make all congregations pretty much the same. First, don't mention tithing. Second, if you mention tithing, leave an opening for a soft and gentle definition. Use the term "sacrificial giving" as a substitute for tithing—even though sacrificial giving may imply something quite opposite to tithing.

Then, always schedule the stewardship season after Labor Day, but a little before Thanksgiving. No preacher wants to get the crass messages of Christian giving confusingly mixed with the warm feeling of the Pilgrims' Thanks Giving. This is always a difficult scheduling balance, since the stewardship season must come toward the end of the year to allow the church the necessary time for budget approval before January. The difficulty is even more pronounced, since more than likely the top line of the budget is the minister's call, reflecting a long deserved increase in salary. Right off the bat, any stewardship message is received as a self-serving plea by the preacher for a pay increase. (Refer back to the Money-Grabbing reason.) So, stewardship season is usually slipped into the first week of October—preferably at the Wednesday night prayer supper.

The stewardship season is an exercise to give obligatory recognition to the discipline of Christian stewardship through the use of adroit flanking maneuvers. This ambiguity is understood by the membership through cultural guidelines that have withstood the test of time for the local congregation. The purpose is clarified with the ultimate production of an annual budget validating another successful stewardship season. Well done. Satisfaction all around. For any of these common reasons, it's a wonder that stewardship is mentioned at all.

Introduction

I'm not saying that our Pastor Dorr was concerned about these common traps, but our congregation did have a long hiatus from one stewardship message to another a few years back. During that drought, I thought to myself, "I believe Stewart can help out." I thought I could help out in a number of ways.

First, we have 52 Sunday services a year, and if only one service is on stewardship, then that's less than 2%. If I can publish a short message 12 times a year, this will give our congregation an 18.75% chance to receive the God's stewardship promises. This approaches Jesus' stewardship teaching standard of about 30% and boosts our church's awareness factor by 800%. (Okay, you can see that deep down I am a numbers nut, but a very poor statistician. Anyway, I figure more is better, and I can help do more.)

Second, we can erase the idea of thinking about stewardship only during a certain season. Stewardship messages can be during any time of the year. I can have a stewardship message all year round. That's the way it should be. I'll admit that one of my biggest dilemmas was deciding which month to start my series. Of course I chose October…the first week of October. I never said I was courageous.

Third, I hoped to reach the entire congregation with a meaningful message. Peter wrote, "Humble yourselves, therefore, under God's mighty hand, that he may lift you up in due time" (1 Pet. 5:6). I read this as a message not for the humble, but for the proud. The proud should be lifted up. In our eyes, each of us is the rich young ruler of the Gospels. We are the patriarchal benefactors. At least we guard our personal wealth like we are. So, God's message for Christian stewardship is for the young careerist and for the industrial mogul equally: *"Humble yourselves."* My stewardship messages are meant for you.

THE FOUR BASICS OF
CHRISTIAN STEWARDSHIP

If you're looking for a "how-to" instruction book for personal economic gain, this is not it. There are enough secular books to help you with how to save money, invest wisely, generate wealth, preserve wealth, and conquer many other personal financial issues. Many of these are of fleeting value. If that statement needs proof, then find a popular book from a decade or so ago. Most are hopelessly irrelevant for today's lifestyles and financial options. The Bible's message is timeless. So, I hope my book offers a "what-if" approach. "What-if" Christians experience a new growth and a revitalization in the stewardship discipline.

I wrote these articles over the course of a couple of years—somewhat as they occurred to me. I tried to be seasonal in many cases. In presenting them to you, I have divided them into four major categories rather than in the chronological order of their publishing. My main themes are Christian stewardship as Worship, Service, Tithing and Prosperity. I have tried to be consistent with these groupings, but, of course, there is overlap.

I trust that you will appreciate my illustrations of these four basics in the following messages. You can read these privately or share them in your Sunday school classroom. If the stewardship committee actually wants to do something this year, the purchase of a few copies for the church library might be appropriate. You can publish individual articles in your church's publications. You have implicit permission to do so, but before you print them, you should check with my publisher first. If you publish them in any form which you intend to commercialize, then you owe a royalty through the publisher. Don't feel threatened by that pecuniary demand. My church will receive the benefits of this royalty and will be wise stewards to the glory of God.

Stewart R. Shipp
Peachtree Corners

Chapter One

WORSHIP

First and foremost, Christian stewardship is worship. Your worship is a response to God and enriches your relationship with God. I can encourage you to worship, but no one can make you worship. I can't tell you how much to worship or when to worship. I strongly feel that Christian giving is the hardest discipline of worship for 21st century Americans. We are a society that praises financial gain. Dollars have become "points" in this self-indulgent praise game. No competitor wants to take points off the board by simply giving them away. Our society doesn't provide for us to cede these gains, and certainly not in the privacy of our worship. Yet, I believe that if we withhold our giving, we are saying that we would rather have the praises of our fellow man, than to grow in our relationship with God. Our worship is then directed toward our assets. That can't be good.

God seeks our growing relationship with Him. He seeks our love. He seeks our praises. He seeks our worship. I don't have the mind of God, but the Bible tells us that He seeks our trust in Him. Stewardship, as an element of our worship, cultivates that trust. God merits it. It's for us to understand that and build it into our relationship with God.

A Personalized Worship Service

I love Sunday morning worship service here in Peachtree Corners. The routine is established and familiar. I stand and sit in unison with the rest of the congregation. I sing the hymnal songs penned years ago. I affirm my convictions on cue, either by memory or by following the bulletin. I listen silently to prayers of invocation, thanksgiving, supplication and praise along with the rest of the congregation. The talents of the musicians inspire me. I open the Bible to the appropriate Scripture. I listen to the sermon while assimilating personal applications. I depart after the benediction with mutual salutations and good wishes among my friends. Every part of the service is a very touching component for the wholeness of my worship. Each is personal. I feel a touch of heaven, perhaps, but certainly a special, personal relationship with the living Lord, Jesus Christ, my Savior.

I consider the Sunday worship to be *my* worship service. Yet, as I have described, very little is conducted at my initiative. For the most part, my personal joy is a reaction to what others have prepared for me. I worship as a responsive member of the church's corporate body. There is only one event in that whole hour that gives much latitude for personalizing *my* worship service. I have one chance to come before God with my creativity. That moment is when the tithes and offerings are collected and presented to the Lord. At that point, it's between Him and me. I alone know the blessings God has given me, and I can respond accordingly. With a humble spirit, I can say, "God, this offering is my personal worship to You. I am setting aside part of my resources to glorify You." My offering is part of my worship.

Yes, I rejoice that I can participate with others in the offering, and I am grateful for the total gifts that the corporate church body brings forth. Together we can pay for the staff, pay for activities, and pay for ministries. My individual offering alone could fund none of these, for sure. I am grateful for the opportunity for my personal worship role, regardless of what others are giving. It's not about totals; it's about a relationship.

What I have described would be a marvelous weekly experience, except for the fact that it is really not quite true. Too often I see the offering as an obligatory commercial break about halfway through the hour. There are those Sundays between paydays that I usually skip the offering altogether. The bank account is a little strained on the Sunday right before my taxes are due, too. The commission check will come in a week or two, and then I promise to catch up big-time. Oops, I forgot my offering envelope. I didn't bring a check. I could go on and on. But, what opportunities I am missing. If I gave consistently every week, would my worship glorify the Lord more? Wouldn't it be a more complete experience if I gave an offering of worship every Sunday, rather than larger amounts only periodically? Sure, by the end of the year the church budget comes out the same, so who notices, what does it matter? Would the congregation notice a difference? Would the world see a difference? Would I be different? God knows.

Stewart R. Shipp
Peachtree Corners

So We Give…

The Sundays between Thanksgiving and Christmas are traditionally a time to catch up our annual giving to the church. I thought that as a November message I would offer my encouragement for us to consider as we budget our year-end giving. Within the limited space available, I provide a list of otherwise endless reasons that we may consider giving a little extra this year.

- For we are extolled to build up treasures in heaven rather than on earth…so we give.
- For we know that we can't take it with us…so we give.
- For we remember something about casting our bread upon the waters…so we give.
- For we hear testimonies about the abundant blessings promised by God…so we give.
- For we have been blessed with good harvests…so we give.
- For we know that that we just don't have enough time to give our time…so we give.
- For our talents are not nearly as good as a lot of others and our talents probably wouldn't make a difference anyway…so we give.
- For we promised a few months ago that we would give anything if we didn't have to work in the nursery ever again…so we give.
- For we know the church budget is prepared annually and it helps everyone if the books are closed with as many receipts as possible…so we give.
- For the Internal Revenue Service only recognizes tax deductions during the year they were given, not the year they were once intended…so we give.

- For our boss told us to anticipate a year-end bonus…so we give.
- For we heard both political parties promising a better economy…so we give.
- For our giving makes us feel good and this holiday we want to feel good…so we give.
- For the church has to spend so much money to make the holiday season special…so we give.
- For our sentiments to continue the traditional spirit of Thanksgiving and Christmas…so we give.

Okay, I'll admit that some of these reasons are a little unwarranted. Even so, there have been times when some of these reasons have at least crossed my mind, and maybe motivated my giving. This Thanksgiving, I encourage each of us to give with another reason in mind. Let's be mindful of a reason for giving that God considered important.

- "For God so loved the world that He gave his only Son, that whoever believes in Him shall not perish but have eternal life" (John 3:16).

So God gave. He loves us. We are His reasons. Sounds unwarranted, doesn't it?

Thanksgiving is an act of worship…so give.

Stewart R. Shipp
Peachtree Corners

Church Books Reveal That Offerings Are Not Needed

I had a chance to review the Church books recently. With all the fuss about spending, slipping budgets, and under funded capital accounts, I found it refreshing to find that no more giving is needed and we don't have to give a penny more. Praise the Lord, I'm sure this comes as a relief to many of you, despite the concerns of Floy, our treasurer. Oh, don't get me wrong, I wasn't privy to see the Church *financial* books; that's not my job. I have only been reviewing those sixty-six books from Genesis to Revelation: the Holy Bible. Those sixty-six Church books give a real clear indication that our giving is *not* needed and we *don't* have to give anymore to accomplish God's work. This may be good news for your personal financial budgets.

Despite this good news, I know that some of you still want to give to keep our building and grounds in good shape. There's always something to buy, equipment to repair, and supplies to replenish. But the Church books are clear that our Heavenly Father has a good handle on creating things and replenishing them without our contributions. I point to his construction of Mount Everest and the Milky Way galaxy to give me confidence that our sanctuary structure is within His measure. He could create several just like it anywhere He wants. Yet, for those inclined to give toward our property maintenance, such gifts are pleasing to God. Our church officers will accept those offerings and prayerfully apply them as you direct. However, clearly God doesn't need Building Funds and you really don't have to give them. God's work will be done.

Despite this good news, there are those who still want to support our worldwide missions, our neighborhood outreach programs, our own Christian Education programs, and the education of missionaries and pastors at Erskine College (our church supported college). Again, the Church books record that for centuries the Holy Spirit has been relentlessly bringing souls to the saving grace of Jesus Christ and revealing the nature of God to the world without mention of any financial assistance from you or me. The Books indicate that this pattern is sure to continue without our contributions. Yet, for those moved to give to our missions, such gifts are pleasing to God. Our church officers will accept offerings and prayerfully apply them as you direct. But clearly God doesn't need Mission Funds, and you really don't have to give them. God's work will be done.

Despite this good news, some of you still want to give benevolently for the caring and nurturing of our congregation, our community, and our world. There are many ways we can do so. Our budget is full of the ministries receiving our benevolences. For those desiring to give toward our benevolent missions, such gifts are pleasing to God. Our church officers will accept those offerings and prayerfully apply them as you direct. Jesus loves all the children of the world, and the Bible tells us so. How can we presume that our benevolence will add one iota to the love Jesus has shown to the world, even to die for us? Clearly God doesn't need Love and Benevolence Funds, and you really don't have to give them. God's work will be done.

Because of the enduring Good News revealed by the Church books to us, some of you will still want to give offerings as worship of adoration, praise and thanksgiving to the Eternal, Omniscient, Omnipresent, Steadfast, Sovereign, Merciful, Righteous, Loving God—The Father, the Son and the Holy Spirit. Such gifts of adoration, praise and thanksgiving are pleasing to God...according to the Church books.

Stewart R. Shipp
Peachtree Corners

What's All the Cheering About?

Collegetown, USA–The University's athletic director announced that although football season ticket sales were sold out again this year, there was a general lack of enthusiasm among the fans. Usually the sellout was completed by early summer; this year's season tickets were still available by late July.

The scuttlebutt around campus is that the last few years' dismal records have dampened the spirits of the alumni and fans. Several years ago, with the undefeated season and treasured national championship still on their minds, the fans cheered all week long—not just at game time. Winning was expected. According to the information director, this mood swing is not expected to have an impact on the athletic budget since ticket sales and donations are continuing as budgeted.

It's just that the fans are merely going through the motions. Supporting the home team on Saturday is what they've done for generations, and the tradition appears to continue, albeit unenthusiastically. The head coach observed that everybody cheers for a winner, but a few defeats can certainly change the atmosphere. At least the loyal fans are thankful for the memories and support the team accordingly.

Okay, you may think that I've gone way out on a limb, and I'm a bit too wrapped up in college football. Bear with me. Hopefully I've set the stage for the following message.

Paul wrote, "Each should give what he has decided in his heart to give, not reluctantly or under compulsion, for God loves a cheerful giver" (2 Cor. 9:7). Truly, I've wrestled with the intentions of this passage for many years. Yes, we feel good when we see God's blessings flow in our lives, and we are thankful that we can give a portion to God in return. I'm sure that God appreciates our gifts as an expression of our good feelings. God appreciates a thankful giver, I'm sure. But I'm thinking that "feeling good" and "cheering" are two different levels of enthusiasm.

An undefeated football season, even with a limited number of fumbles, a few interceptions, and not many missed tackles is really something to cheer about. After all, nobody is perfect. The Bible describes our Creator as incomparable, glorious, unconquerable—yes, undefeatable. His seasons are eternal. His righteousness is unblemished and without error. He is perfect. We are his loyal children. What's not to cheer?

Our giving without compulsion or reluctance is a worthy deed that Paul urges us to pursue. Our faithful stewardship as a traditional Christian discipline is admirable and will reap promised rewards from our Father. Our gifts of thanksgiving for the blessings God has given us are pleasing to Him, and He will continue to pour His blessings upon us. However, He especially treasures our enthusiastic, cheerful gifts recognizing Him as the undefeatable, incomparable, almighty God. Such cheering is not about us, not about our good feelings, not about our loyalty, but they are for Him. Let us cheer on. Glory, glory to our Father.

Stewart R. Shipp
Peachtree Corners

Setting Up a Trust Program

They say George Washington studied the scripture and prayed each morning for two hours. He also concluded each day with a brief reading of scripture and a prayer. We have seen portraits of our first president kneeling in prayer at Valley Forge during the bleak months of the Revolutionary War. He began his inauguration and concluded his farewell addresses with prayer. There has been no greater influence on the American heritage than George Washington. Apparently, there was no greater influence on George Washington than God Almighty. George Washington trusted in the Living God as his Shepherd, his Counselor, and his Steadfast Rock. When we celebrate the birth of our independent nation, this is a comforting thought.

During the long history of our nation, a particular series of historical events seem completely out of character with today's political culture. Did you know that as early as 1861 the US Mint produced coins inscribed with the motto, "In God We Trust"? In 1957, Congress approved, the President signed, and the Supreme Court has not challenged the printing of all our paper currency with those same words: "In God We Trust." It's fitting that George Washington's portrait and that motto are both on the one-dollar bill.

All of this gets me thinking about my giving habits. Here's what I'm thinking and I'm sure this happens to you, too. Situations arise, apart from our regular giving, when we are asked to give but are not financially prepared to do so at that moment. A few situations come to mind, like our special benevolence offerings each quarter, the youth Sunday collections, or even those off-schedule Sundays between our paydays. I usually pass the offering plate along, or put in a mere dollar. I'm thinking…this mere dollar bill can be more than it seems. Can I make this dollar bill a faith statement? Here's my plan for the next occasion. I'll pull out my wallet, select a bill with Washington's portrait, turn it over, and quietly contemplate, "In God We Trust." Then I am going to fold the bill so the motto faces up as I place it in the offering plate. I'm hoping that this changes these incidental offerings to a stronger personal commitment to trust in God. I hope it reminds me that I can trust God enough to give a dollar. I can trust God in my relationships; I can trust God for life itself. Yet it's been so hard to trust God with my financial assets, and I hope to change that…even if it takes a symbolic dollar bill.

There's no way for our church to meet our financial objectives with a plate of only one-dollar bills. But what would happen if we sincerely put our trust in God with every offering? God doesn't depend on our finances, whether for one dollar or for one million dollars. The quantitative difference has more meaning to us than it does to Him. Quantitatively, both are insignificant compared to His bounty. The significance of our giving is our commitment of trusting in Him. The giving is worship for Him.

I submit that George Washington's trust in God rewarded him, as well as our great nation. Although my life long endeavors will never equate to that great man, I'm trusting God that my life and my community will prosper to some degree through this trust. Be thankful for our national heritage of trusting in God. It could change your life.

Stewart R. Shipp
Peachtree Corners

Letter to Stewart Shipp

Dear Stewart Shipp,

I have a problem with dealing with my mother. Don't get me wrong, I love Mother, and I know that she loves me. In fact, I couldn't ask for more. She, of course, gave me life, nurtured me, taught me, and continues to give me so much more than I deserve.

I could tell endless stories about her. My earliest school memories are her being with me when I studied for tests. Before each and every test, she would come to my desk and steady my nerves. When I was out of college, I asked her to come with me on my first job interview, and she did. She was right there with me, and she reminded me of how I should act and what I could say. I didn't get that job, but she comforted me so much anyway. With her guidance I finally got a job that was just right for me. When my daughter was in surgery after an accident, Mom assured me that everything would be all right. It was amazing. The surgeon said he credited Mother's presence as the source of my daughter's survival. He told me he gained strength and inspiration from Mom's being with him in that operating room. When my wife and I were having our difficulties, Mom was a source of wisdom for us both, and we honor her for that. It's great to have a Mom that loves me so much.

Don't get me wrong, Stewart, I'm a good son. I adore her immensely. I go see her every week. My friends and I go over to her house every Sunday. We talk about all the things she has done and share our concerns with her. We sing songs together that we have written just for her. We try to focus all our attention on her when we are with her.

My problem is that I have a hard time with giving her gifts. First of all, Mom has everything. Truly she is wealthy. I couldn't give her anything that she doesn't already have. You name it…she owns it. Furthermore, I have several well-to-do brothers and sisters that give her fairly lavish gifts all the time. They seem to be the "go-to" people when Mom points out special needs for the neighbors. Stewart, I can't compete with these brothers and sisters. And besides, it seems like she will just go out and give them back more than they gave. What's the point of that? Since what they give comes back to them multiplied, I'm beginning to suspect their motives. Maybe later, when I get in better financial shape, I'll step up to their level. I really hope to be like them someday—someday, in a few more years.

Mother knows my financial condition. Right now, anything more than a small gift every now and then would be a big deal for my budget. It's a struggle out here in the real world. Frankly, I don't think Mom has any experience with the financial burdens I carry. I ask her advice often, but how could she know much about my job requirements? I just don't think she has it together when it comes to understanding my personal finances. Stewart, I'm just not where I want to be right now. It seems the harder I try, the more I get behind. Mom should understand my efforts and understand that my gifts are from a big heart but also a strained pocketbook.

Stewart, I need your advice about giving to Mom. First, am I obligated to give anything to Mom? Is there a good rule-of-thumb about how much I should spend? Is there a certain percentage, like tipping, although there's no way I could give her 15%. I can't treat her like a waitress. Can a simple "thank you" be enough?

I'm thinking that a larger, token gift to show my love every once in a while might be better than smaller gifts routinely. But you know how difficult that is, don't you? I guess I could give something. Deep down in my heart I guess I know I should give even more than something. I would just have to adjust so much...my budget, my priorities, my lifestyle, and everything that means anything to me. Questions, questions, questions. What's a poor soul to do?

Dear Poor Soul,

I've heard of someone else in a similar situation, but I just can't quite place it. Let me ask around to find out what others might do with someone like your mom. I'll get back to you with an answer.

Stewart R. Shipp
Peachtree Corners

How Rich and Wise Were Those Rich Wise Men?

Christmas is a time for giving, and giving is the purpose of Christian stewardship, isn't it? It's better to give than to receive, right? This is hard for me to say, but giving is not the goal either.

The Magi who came to Bethlehem with gifts to Jesus began the Christmas tradition of giving. They brought gold, myrrh, and incense from their treasures. Folklore leads us to think that there were three of them. Their familiarity with the Old Testament indicates that they had access to Hebrew writings left in Babylon after the Exile. These particular Magi were keen academics and extraordinarily fortunate. They not only deciphered Old Testament predictions that most Israelites had missed, but they sighted the very star in the direction of Bethlehem proclaiming this prophecy. Each Christmas we celebrate them as three rich kings ("three wise men").

I've heard that it's good to be rich. Look at those Magi. These men traveled a distance comparable to going from Peachtree Corners to Miami. They traveled for days—maybe months—over terrain that was mostly desert. It's safe to assume they rode camels. Rich men rode camels back then. Whether or not they traveled with an entourage is not clear. Their wardrobes must have been ostentatious enough to get Herod's attention. It's a fair assumption that he saw them to be rich. I'm not sure that I do. Imagine you're on your way to Miami, driving maybe 70-75 mph on cruise control with the air-conditioner humming, an Icee in the cup holder, and Merle's greatest hits on the CD. You've got about three or four hours left to travel. Then, out of the blue, the traffic slows to a crawl, and after several miles of this you see three guys dressed in gaudy woolen robes up ahead, riding camels and carrying tote bags of gold, myrrh and incense.

As you merge into the single file attempting to pass them, you may think they are rich, but I'm not sure I do. History considers them rich, but I guess that just depends on who's doing the comparing.

I'm already too harsh. Let's give them their due. The Magi spent a lot of time studying the Hebrew Scriptures. They identified the precursors to the divine incarnation, evaluated the apparent advent of this incarnation, and then struck out over the desert to prove their hypothesis. They found the star that hadn't been there before, leading them to Bethlehem, and they arrived in time to see, or at least hear of, the greatest pageant in mankind's history. Herald angels, trembling shepherds, awesome lights, and a newborn baby…'tis enough to make a church music director shiver. They came to the house of the child and his mother, Mary. They presented their gifts, fell to their knees, and worshipped Jesus, king of the Jews. The Bible says, "They returned to their country by another route" (Matt. 2:12). They went home. They left. They went about their normal business. Could this be right? They returned to their country. Were these wise men really wise?

They did give to Jesus. The three gifts imply that they knew his purpose in the world for kingship, sacrifice and resurrection. They gave, but apparently came away with nothing. Nothing changed. I'm astonished that these men could intellectually validate the power of and personally experience the reality of the God of all heaven and earth coming to live among them, yet then leave the country to go about their business as usual. Their gifts were magnificent and worthy of Biblical recording, but as mere transactions, nothing more. Giving is worship, but sometimes giving is just giving. For centuries, they have been called wise men, but I think that just depends on who's doing the comparing.

Again, I'm too harsh. If this coming February is like other years, I will find myself paying off the Christmas bills, or looking at a few Christmas photos, or reconciling my cancelled Christmas offering check. These records show what I heard, what I saw, what I gave, and how I worshipped. By mid-winter, only these records of transactions will remain. It will occur to me that I'm just like those Magi. I have returned home. I have returned to business as usual. The Christmas spirit of giving has waned to only the routine of writing another offering check. Christmas is worship, but sometimes Christmas is just Christmas. I'd like to say I'm a wise man, and perhaps I am, but I guess that just depends on who's doing the comparing.

Enjoy your Christmas worship…all next year.

Stewart R. Shipp
Peachtree Corners

A Resolution for the Tender-Hearted

It's time again for those New Year's resolutions. I will probably stick to my usual resolutions. Every year, I resolve to read the Bible straight through from cover to cover. I am always pleased with that resolution. It would be a good thing to do. It would be good for me, and it would occupy a whole year at a good reading pace. Yet, despite my intentions, I know that I won't get past Leviticus.

To make it easier this year, I'm resolving to read past the first ten chapters of Leviticus. I know I can do that, because I've reached that point every year before, even though it took me the better part of the year. It's not that I read so slowly, it's that Leviticus is so tedious. The book is an instruction manual for the Levite priests. It opens with the directions for ritual sacrificing of bulls, goats, birds, and lambs. (Yawn.) The passages describe in great detail these rituals for the burnt offering, grain offering, fellowship offering, thanksgiving offering, sin offering, and guilt offering. (Yawn, again.) As Christians we believe that Jesus, as the unblemished Lamb of God, was the final sacrifice. Thanks be to God, we don't have to present livestock to a priest anymore; yet, these passages still remain in the Holy Book, if only to present a formidable hurdle for reading straight through the Bible. Arcane though they are, there is one repetitive phrase that springs from these verses, denoting an intriguing difference in the offerings. That, my friends, is the essence of this month's message.

For the burnt offerings of thanksgiving and fellowship, the instructions end with the declaration that these offerings burning on the altar give an "aroma pleasing to the Lord." On the other hand, for the sin and guilt offerings, there is no mention of an aroma, pleasing or otherwise. Such a response may startle some. Even with God's heavy schedule of running the universe, He can take the time to be pleased with aromas, even to differentiating one from other very similar smells.

This, in turn, got me thinking about nice things like flowers and my wife. (Your mind does tend to wander when you read Leviticus.) Back when I was a young married man, I regret that I never understood my wife's *flower thing*. Any flowers at all were given only for birthdays or anniversaries. It's an odd thing, but I can remember the kids bringing home their school drawings of flowers. With a tenderhearted smile on her face, she lovingly hugged them, told them how beautiful the drawings were, and imitated smelling those pictures. They seemed to have a particularly pleasing aroma, more than your typical crayon smell. Later, for no particular reason, I picked up some flowers from a street vendor. There was no anniversary, no birthday, and no exceptional feeling of guilt. (I'm Presbyterian, so there is always some guilt.) She couldn't have been more pleased. There was little if any difference between these flowers and others that I had brought home before for special occasions. I can still hear her saying how wonderful they smelled, even though I'm still not sure that daffodils have a smell. I'm grateful she is so tenderhearted.

In Leviticus, God accepted all the burnt offerings. With the wonders of His love, He accepted the sin sacrifices and guilt sacrifices, and true to His word He forgave. I'm intrigued, though, that He was especially pleased with the aroma of those offerings presented with thanksgiving and adoration. So again, my mind wanders. Generally, my giving to God is motivated by the requirements at hand. We have to meet the church budget, so I give. The community has needs, so I give. I'm striving to tithe, so I give a little more. I have a sense that God will return blessings as promised, so I give expectantly. Maybe there is a little bit of guilt, so I give with contrition. I'm sure God appreciates these offerings with His abounding love. Yet, every now and then gifts are presented for no other reason than for thanksgiving and worship, for fellowship with God, for simply the love of God. No one else knows of the motivation, only God. I pray that these gifts have a special aroma pleasing to God. I'm grateful He is so tenderhearted.

In the New Testament, Paul writes to the Ephesians, "Christ loved us and gave Himself up for us, as a fragrant offering and sacrifice to God" (Eph. 5:2). Our Savior gave for love. Without Leviticus, I would miss another example of how truly tenderhearted our God is.

This year I resolve that I will bring my wife some flowers, that I will read the entire book of Leviticus, and that at least one of my offerings will have an aroma pleasing to God.

Stewart R. Shipp
Peachtree Corners

Chapter Two

SERVICE

Stewardship is service, for we are using our resources to glorify God. Much like "...faith without deeds is dead" (James 2:26), so is a church without Christian stewardship service. A church is to do God's work with the accumulation of its gifts of time and talents, as well as those financial gifts resulting from its worship. Worshipful giving is a response to God. Stewardship service, meaning Christian ministries and programs, is the fruit of worshipful giving. It should be so easy to balance the two.

Unfortunately, the balance is often lost when a church's service agenda is beyond that of its worshipful giving. Worshipful giving should not be a response to service goals. Since there are so many ministries and programs a church could do, there is a tendency for church officials to define service ministries and programs first and then prayerfully hope that the congregation can support them by simply giving more. This generally results in churches reaching beyond their capabilities and falling short of their intended goals. Such giving-for-service not only causes frustration among the congregation, but also disfigures stewardship worship. Unfortunately, worshipful giving is often transformed from a response to God into a mandate from the budget committee.

On the other side, there can be an imbalance when a church accumulates excessive funds from its tithes and offerings. Under the banner of fiscal prudence, church officers may direct that surpluses be built up for future, yet unknown events. Sadly, this belies a church's message to the congregation to trust the Lord for the future. It prompts the congregation to question its personal giving disciplines, seeing that worshipful giving only builds deposits in a local bank. Please don't mistake my message. I'm not talking about the accumulating of designated funds for known expenditures, like building funds or scholarship funds. I'm concerned that so many established churches have such large cash finances, when the work of the Lord could be fulfilled around them. They are preparing for the future, but the future never seems to come.

Our stewardship service requires us to be diligent stewards with the time, talents, and financial resources that we presently have, rather than those resources we pray that we might someday have, or fear that we might someday need.

STEWARDSHIP TIME-MACHINE DISCOVERED

Time is a truly remarkable creation. It's hard to comprehend that before the creation, there was no Time[1]. We've never lived without Time. Yet, God did create Time; the Bible tells us so. Time serves as a useful tool for the rest of God's creation. Many smart people spend a lot of time trying to figure out how far back time goes and where God was at the time of the beginning—or even what time God began. I'm not one to interfere with their intellectual musings, but I find their endeavors baseless.

Imagine a carpenter "creating" a table using a measuring tape. The tape is a useful tool, both for his table making and later descriptions of his table. It would allow him to make the table with precision, plus it gives the table user a perspective for how many people can sit around it, or how much can be placed on top of it. The carpenter made a measuring tape to help make his table. The carpenter's customer wouldn't ask, "So, Carpenter, where were you before ½ inch? Are you the same at 8-feet-3-inches as you are going to be at the end of the twenty-foot tape?" How could a carpenter answer such nonsense? His creation uses that measuring tape, but he is outside both the table and the tape.

We are quite fortunate that God did create Time. Not only does Time prevent every thing from running together (as an old Ziggy cartoon implied); it also serves God's purposes for man's stewardship over this earthly creation. Time is a meter—a meter to keep up with the recurring cycles. With Time, we know when to go to church, when to go get the morning newspaper,

---

[1] In certain phrases I have capitalized "Time" because as God's creation it's a resource fully created. Otherwise, as a passage along a spectrum of events, it's merely "time", a concept that we humans are compelled to reference according to our place within that spectrum. Never mind, that's for another book.

when to expect snow, and when someone has missed another anniversary. Time is also a measurement, such as miles-per-hour and feet-per-second.

Also, Time is a unit of capacity. "How much time do I have to write this?" I can't imagine how we could ever live without Time.

We seldom have enough of this resource, Time. We might be able to do certain tasks in a year's time, but most of the time we only have a week or so to do them. Recently, I had a little time on my hands, so I began to contemplate just how we could do a year's work in a week's time. I must say, I have discovered a great Time Machine that can be a remarkable stewardship tool. Before I send my idea off to the Patent Office, I'll share it with you.

I started with the fact that our congregation has about 350 members. Collectively, by next week we will have lived an aggregate 350 weeks. That's seven years of living. Imagine what we could do in seven years. Furthermore, in a year's time, we will have lived 350 years. Think of all the souls who have come to Christ in the past 350 years. Think of all the church has done in the past 350 years. We should be able to accomplish so much in these 350 years given to us this coming year. What a powerful resource God has given the church body. I've discovered a Time Machine, and it's right here in the pews with us.

Okay, Stewart, snap out of it. I've mixed the concept of Time's *meter* with Time's *capacity*. There is a difference between an hour and a man-hour. I apologize to you readers for leading you down such a spurious path. Goodness, to expect that we can get 350 years of work with 350 people in a year's time would require an unearthly management coordination effort. First, my machine would need a strong, wise, visionary central operator with a rock solid objective. Then, the information flow for such micromanagement to each person would be inconceivable, even with today's information and communication technology. My machine would need a huge broadband spectrum for the necessary bulk of information flow required to and from our member operating units. The machine must have instantaneous connectivity to a virtual limitless database, managed with mega-mega hertz operating speed. Then we need this central processor to instantly recycle the perfect operational information back to the relevant operating units in simultaneous coordination. Alas, I've discovered a Time-Machine right here in front of my face, but it's too complex. Who can operate it? Lo, Christ Jesus has been doing so since the creation of Time through the connectivity of prayer.

How great God is! He has an eternal vision for His creation beyond our imaginations. He has appointed us as stewards of His earthly creation. Thankfully, He has given each of us special talents for such an assignment. He has even leveraged our individual resources with the collection of gifts in the church body, which He heads. He has the power. He has the wisdom. He has given us the time. We need only look to Him for time management. Pray to the Lord for His guidance of our church as one body. In a single year as the body of Christ acting together in the will of God, we can do years and years of service for His honor and glory.

There's no time like the present.
Steward R. Shipp
Peachtree Corners

Of Katrina and Things and Time and Stewardship

I'm writing this article during the first week after Hurricane Katrina. The destructive aftermath is too great for me to get my arms around. From what I can see through the eyes of the 24-hour newscasts, these may be the worst of times as civil disorder emerges, yet these are the best of times as human compassion is revealed. However, my objective is not social discourse but stewardship.

I could isolate my thoughts to environmental stewardship. Who is Man that God has given us this earthly dominion? Have we tried too hard, or not hard enough? Are we responsible for Katrina's destructiveness through our poor global stewardship, or have we mastered so much about our dominion that we have lessened its destructive forces to only the degree that we see. In the face of Katrina, the immensity of our environmental task is too great for me to get my arms around for this message.

Perhaps I should write about the stewardship of generosity. There may have been failures to get immediate relief to the victims, but there has been no lack of generous intentions. Americans are generous people. I assert that it's Christian giving that pushes this admirable trait to its heights. I'll admit that Christians don't have a lock on big-heartedness, but it seemed to me that Christian organizations, and Christian leaders in secular organizations, led the post-Katrina efforts. Christians have been giving aid for centuries. It's the fruit of who we are. The out-stretched arms of Christian giving have been open for generations. But we are at our best when we do it for the glory of the Lord. And the Lord surely blesses us for that. Yet, I'm not going to write about either of those stewardship angles.

"You can't take it with you" is often heard, but Katrina gave that bromide an unexpected twist to the hurricane survivors, as things were taken away without taking them. With Katrina, we see that things and time reached a sudden finality not usually experienced this side of death. The citizens of the Gulf Coast either evacuated and left their belongs before the hurricane, or stayed to watch their belongs roar away with the winds and water. Except for a hastily loaded pickup truck, or a garbage bagful of survival items, they couldn't take things with them in the short time available for escape. Their post-catastrophe glazed expressions virtually shouted out, "What's it all about? All the things I've spent my time working for are gone." Their things had abandoned them and were now worthless, and, now, the time spent to accumulate them seemed to be wasted, too.

Things and time. God gave us both, and we have come to treasure both. Yet every now and then we are abruptly reminded of just how unreliable these treasures are. With the speed of a hurricane, we can be out of time and out of things. Yet, since God gave us both, they must have value, mustn't they? Certainly they do. They have their most value, and really their only lasting value, when we use them to honor and glorify God. Through our stewardship, our time dedicated to the Lord is memorialized, and things given in the name of the Lord become blessings. God wants us to enjoy things and time, and we should enjoy his gifts. But merely gathering and keeping things around is not enough. God is pleased when things and time are presented for His glory.

With compassion for our neighbors on the Gulf Coast, I trust they know that the immensity of the circumstances is not too large for the Most Powerful in the universe. He has His arms around it all, and He has His arms around them, as well. We can take that with us.

Stewart R. Shipp
Peachtree Corners

DON'T GIVE THOSE JOKERS ANOTHER DIME

Maybe you have heard this sort of thing, too. Not long ago a member of another church complained to me, "I'm not going to give those Jokers one more dime, if they keep wasting it on…" I didn't hear which ministry he thought was a waste. Alas, I wanted to tell him, "Don't complain to me, buddy; tell it to those Jokers." Yet, since I'm not one to waste my money either, I replied, "I'm with you, friend. I really don't want to give my dime to any Jokers either."

I decided to do a little research here at Peachtree Corners to discover if Jokers have anything to do with my church finances. On the Sunday of my investigation, our pastor, as a part of worship, led the congregation in prayer to give our tithes and offerings to God. (He didn't mention the Jokers.) Then the ushers, possibly under the direction of the Jokers, came forward to collect the dime that I had placed in my offering envelope. The pastor offered a prayer thanking God and praying that our gifts would be used in accordance to God's will. Then the ushers, not at all like Jokers, took the offering out of sight.

My sleuthing took me to a side room down a church hall, where two apparent henchmen for the Jokers carefully counted the offerings received. Then, they deposited the funds and gave the Sunday report to Floy, our church treasurer. Floy was then my prime suspect for Joker-ship. Yet he had been elected by our congregation and had served for many years. No one in the church doubted his absolute integrity, so the notorious Jokers were at this point still unidentified.

That particular Sunday, Floy wrote out some checks. He paid for things that keep up the place, like the light bill, the power bill, and the telephone bill. Surely there may be a Joker or two at those places, but nothing to get alarmed about. He paid for some expenses for our Vacation Bible School and our contribution to the Denominational World-wide Mission ministry. After a while, it was apparent that Floy was conscious of complying with the church budget. My investigation turned to the preparation of that budget. The elusive Jokers were surely behind it.

It took a little while to uncover the budget process, but each year our Deacons, elected by our congregation, have special meetings to prepare a budget for the upcoming year. Line-by-line those folks discuss the budget, its consequences for the church's future, and the commitments to serve the Lord. Soon after, a preliminary budget is presented to our Session. Again, prayer for guidance preceded both deliberations. The Session approved the budget. This procedure is consistent with the Associate Reform Presbyterian Form of Government and long-time Presbyterian traditions. The members of these boards have been elected by our congregation with due consideration for integrity, godliness, and dedication—traits generally not found in Jokers.

Later, before each budget year starts, our treasurer presents the proposed budget to our congregation for approval. Our congregational meeting opens with prayer for guidance. In some years the budget passes without modification, some years unanimously, and sometimes with minority dissent, but it is always approved by us, the congregation.

So here's how my investigation concluded. Our congregation's giving is truly an act of worship and thanksgiving. Each member's giving is an individual relationship with God. Our church body, through an established regimen and seeking guidance from the Holy Spirit, spends these funds to serve God's purposes. Our individual gifts to God become our combined resource to serve God. Together we are God's servants, praying that the monies given to Him are used for His service and glory.

Had I found the Jokers of my friend's complaints? Indeed, I found those Jokers, and we are they. But as for this church, through prayer and long established protocol, we Jokers seek to be trumped by the power of the King, for service and glory to God. Good deal.

Stewart R. Shipp
Peachtree Corners

CHRISTMAS WITH MR. POTATO HEAD

One of my favorite Christmas stories is in Paul's first letter to the Corinthians describing the talents of the Church in terms of a Christmas toy he received when he was a youngster. "The body is a unit, though it is made up of many parts...Now you are the body of Christ and each is a part of it" (1 Cor. 12:12). Okay, maybe I'm a little far-fetched with Paul's imagery, and certainly with the historical possibility of Paul's childhood celebration of Christmas, but whenever I hear that passage, I can't help but reminisce of a Mr. Potato Head I once received for Christmas.

Back then you had to use a real potato, but inside the box were a couple dozen parts: plastic eyes, ears, noses, several pairs of feet and hands, and several hats. On that Christmas, my first arrangements produced rather recognizable variations of Mr. Potato Head. With only those few pieces, I could have made hundreds of ordinary variations of Mr. Potato Head. But, having the mindset of any young boy, I was soon bored with the ordinary and began to experiment with the bizarre. Soon a potato having nothing but eyes emerged. He had blue eyes, brown eyes, big eyes, sad eyes and more. He was an eyeful. Later, parts were gradually lost and broken. The nose parts were the first to vanish entirely. Without a nose part, Mr. Potato Head never looked quite right—even with that ear in the center of his face. When my sister got her own Miss Potato Head, she left all the pieces in the box and just played with the plastic potato that had been added since my gift. (My sister really wasn't that weird, but I need that image to complete this article.)

So, I envision my Mr. Potato Head of long ago when I hear Paul's passage. It's somewhat applicable. First, I think we could say that God has given each church a complete box of parts. Certainly our church has every necessary part. Each part is good at something. With the wide variation of parts, no church has to be exactly like any other church, nor does it have to stay with the same make-up forever. There must be hundreds of variations that any church could undertake with its parts. Second, no matter how gifted one part is, a church body can't depend only on that one part. For example, the eye is a very complex organ. It's focused, it sees things clearly, and it is vigilant. But, a church with only eyes begins to be…well, cockeyed. The nose, on the other hand, has a fairly straightforward task of transferring air to and from the lungs. Occasionally, it's required to detect a smell—a sometimes-disgusting task—and even other times it is a thankless task. Smelling always takes a backseat to seeing, tasting, touching and hearing. But as easy as that nose job is, an ear trying to be a nose just can't pass the smell test. Third, none of the parts do any good remaining in the box. With no parts out of the box, all you have is a stupid potato.

God gave each of us talents. Each of us is good at something. For a Christmas gift to our church this year, let's share our gifts with God's church. We have some really wonderful "eyes" in this church, but they can't do it all. Some things that are easy for one part are impossible for another. Each role is essential, no matter how complex or straightforward. There are enough parts in our church to serve God in ways that we cannot yet imagine, if only all of us would get out of the box. Finally, let's get out of the box on our own. Who are we waiting for? Do we expect a pair of feet to just walk up and ask us to lend an ear?

I dream that sometime next year I will ask a first-time visitor, "What do you think of Peachtree Corners?" I hope that her response will be, "It's a great church. Somebody really knows how to make a wonderful Potato Head Church." That's what I'm talking about, my friends.

Okay, you hand-pieces, let's see some High-Fives all around.

Stewart R. Shipp
Peachtree Corners

Service

STEWART SHIPP IS OFF FOR THE SUMMER

Note From The Editor:

Dear Readers,

We regret to inform you that there will not be a message from Stewart R. Shipp for June. Stewart Shipp, as expected, will be off for the summer. According to our records, Stewart Shipp is always off during the summer.

Pastor Dorr informed us that there is no particular biblical reason for Stewart Shipp to be off every summer. "It's more of a church tradition, rather than doctrine. All through the year, our worship service gives time for Stewart Shipp. We continue to keep this time in the service, even though we know that Stewart Shipp may be off for the summer. In some respects, it will seem like we're just going through the motions without Stewart Shipp involved as usual."

Floy, the church treasurer, assured us that while he hates it, he had prepared for Stewart Shipp to be off just like every other summer. "During the spring I know to cut back our dependence on Stewart Shipp. Then, when Stewart Shipp is off for the summer it's not so drastic. I don't get concerned unless Stewart Shipp hasn't returned by September."

Elder Pooser, the clerk of session, was simply perplexed. "The congregation seems so inspired when Stewart Shipp is in full form. It just doesn't seem like a church without Stewart Shipp."

One deacon lamented, "I can't understand why Stewart Shipp is always off during the summer anyway. It's not like we don't have needs."

Others pointed out that Stewart Shipp is an integral supporter of many of our church ministries. "Yes, we always endure the summer, but we could do so much more throughout the year if we had our familiar Stewart Shipp during the summer, too," Miss Ann, the Christian Education director, pointed out.

Several members were apparently unaware that Stewart Shipp is off every summer. Surprisingly, some have never even been involved with Stewart Shipp at all. "I never knew that Stewart Shipp was such a big deal around here until you told me."

A few even said that Stewart Shipp was not their problem; they had bigger worries out in the real world. An anonymous telephone message summed up that sentiment. "Quit harping about Stewart Shipp. I've got to deal with my own priorities this summer."

We ask you to do what you can to encourage Stewart Shipp to return by July, if not sooner. There are so many things that we rely on Stewart Shipp to do around here. As with others before you, perhaps Stewart Shipp could help you personally, too.

Chimes Editorial Staff
Peachtree Corners

Chapter Three
―――――――――――――――

TITHING

Stewardship is a discipline, and the cornerstone of that discipline is the practice of tithing. Tithing is not a number; tithing is a commitment. Tithing is a response. I'll guess that other than fasting, tithing is the last Christian discipline to be practiced by a maturing Christian. Many never do. It's counter-intuitive. It just seems so illogical, so foreign to modern economic theories. Consequently, it's either redefined or softened or manipulated to fit into the modern American's practices.

Tithing is more that an annual number. Tithing is not a once-a-year discipline; it's an on-going discipline. I would like for my discipline to be not about a ten percent obligation, a ten percent standard, a ten percent goal, or even a ten percent limit. I would like for my tithing discipline to be a consistent and routine occurrence—not a final dash for the goal at a certain time of the year. I would like for my tithing discipline to see that tithing is like other Christian disciplines, not something fully attained, but something we continually strive for like prayer. I pray, but could I pray more? I pray, but do I pray sincerely enough? I pray, but do I pray like He desires me to pray? Does my prayer bring me closer to God? Is my prayer pleasing to God? Any Christian discipline can be substituted in the preceding sentences, but "giving tithes" may be the most difficult substitution. I pray that someday each of us is tithing and that all are striving to grow in our tithing.

I strongly feel that the recipient of our tithes can only be the local church of our worship. Tithing to the local church is the singular way to bring together the worship and service of Christian stewardship—the first two basics of stewardship. The foundation of our committed giving, tithing is a special and perhaps mysterious discipline, but it is transforming. Tithing enhances our worship. It magnifies our service. And, it brings us into closer harmony with the will of our Lord.

Investment Prophet Extols Tithing Profit

We have seen the TV evangelists pleading for our contributions with promises that future blessings will flow our way. We've heard personal testimony from fellow Christians about God's blessings following personal tithes and offerings. We have also read Bible verses that promise us prosperity, multiplying our gifts. Prosperity is a good thing. Yet, to tell you the truth, even with Biblical authority, I have been cautious to mention prosperity resulting from tithing. I can talk about praying with beneficial expectations, but tithing with beneficial expectations is a different matter. Linking tithing with prosperity can be so easily misunderstood. Now, lo and behold, I have come across an unimpeachable authority advocating tithing as a prudent financial practice. *Forbes* is one of today's best business and investment magazines. To my delight, its publisher and columnist, Rich Karlgaard, recently wrote, "Tithing will liberate the tither from financial worry."[1]

Karlgaard cites some other beneficial results of tithing:

- "When I began to tithe, I found a freedom from my possessions. I don't hold onto things as tightly as before."
- "Tithing requires discipline, but that discipline begins to show up unexpectedly in other areas of my life. When I began to tithe, I was able to be more patient with people."
- "Tithing puts you in touch with people's needs—an excellent business habit."
- "When you tithe, you begin to see your role as a steward of resources. You don't engage in wasteful spending."

---

[1] *Forbes*, 2/14/05

He concludes, "Tithing is a duty of faith. One must never tithe with expectations of divine reward." Amen and amen. God bless Rich Karlgaard.

Based upon this business and investment endorsement, will the next rage of the secular world be tithing? I'm not holding my breath for the tithing fad to capture Hollywood, but I do believe the effects would be positive. Doesn't the New Age practitioner experience healing when meditating and praying? Many times they do. Doesn't the public school teacher see a heightened sense of ethical morality in the classroom when the Bible is read? They used to. Can't an atheist enjoy financial benefit from tithing? Probably so, according to *Forbes*.

The Bible affirms Mr. Karlgaard's observations, but with a significant difference. I'll go along with the *Forbes* philosophy. Our tithing will indeed enhance our financial condition, but God intends more than that for us. In Christ, we have a relationship with the true living God. This relationship is not about what we do, but who God is. Our offerings are our worship; offerings are not our investment. Our gifts are our response, not our expectation. Our tithes are for thanksgiving, not for return on investment. We can do nothing worthy of any return. Yet, through the love of the living God, His blessings shall abound. I won't expect it, but I expect it's true. That's the way He is.

> Bring the whole tithe into the storehouse, that there may be food in my house. "Test me in this," says the Lord Almighty, "and see if I will not throw open the floodgates of heaven and pour out so much blessing that you will not have room enough for it."
>
> (Mal. 3:10)

I'll never find better advice in *Forbes*.
Stewart R. Shipp
Peachtree Corners

BE ALL THAT YOU WERE MEANT TO BE

As a veteran I'm very proud of today's armed forces. I'm especially impressed with the resources that our troops bring with them—things like the naval launched missiles, the satellite communications, the night vision goggles, the drone aircraft, and all the rest. The total integration of these resources has made our armed forces a vastly superior military force to whatever nation is second best, and the resources seem to be allocated so effectively. It seems that Army has the resources to be good soldiers; the Navy, good sailors; the Air Force, good airmen; and the Marines, as always, good Marines. To top it off, our men and women have voluntarily obligated themselves to defend our freedom.

Our military is a unit of diverse skills and talents. As diverse as the forces are among the four services, they share one thing in common, and with every veteran since to the Continental Army. Each of us did two things upon entering the service. The first thing we did was to commit our loyalty to our country and the constitution. Without my swearing-in ceremony, the Army wasn't going do a thing for me. My overt commitment was the tip-off that now I was ready to go about the business of being a soldier. The next event was to shear off my hair, strip me down to my skivvies, and stand me in line as a supply sergeant outfitted me with all sorts of paraphernalia. Now, the oath was a mixed bag. There's a sense of great patriotism, but also a certain anxiety. The second step produced a singular feeling for everyone. "Do I look like a fool, or what? Hurry up and get me my gear so I can move on."

Now I don't want to get carried away comparing the human to the divine. The divine is then the more likely to suffer. And I assume that the Army is still laden with "The Right Way, the Wrong Way, and the Army Way," and other banalities of military life. Nothing by man is perfect, but I can't help comparing these experiences with God's perfect plan. As believers we are all citizens of the holy kingdom, and that can never be lost. Yet, I believe God is recruiting us for greater service to Him. He is ready to lead us into that service. We must start with two events. We make a commitment that indicates our trust in His plan for us, and we symbolically cast off our own resources so to be equipped with the resources He provides us for the service He desires of us. In terms of Christian stewardship that commitment, I believe, is the discipline of tithing. When we tithe, we indicate our commitment and our trust. We are saying, "God, I trust you and your promises. I am replacing my desires with your plans." From that time forward we are built up, equipped, and trained to be stewards for the glory of God.

When you join the military, you have given the government some indication about what you want to be, where you want to go, and what you want to do: as the US Army slogan says, *"Be All That You Can Be."* When we trust the Lord, our future is in His hands. It's His plan, not ours. Consequently, for many of us self-reliant types, there's an apprehension that somehow the Lord is going to leave us looking foolish, standing in our metaphoric skivvies, incapable of doing what He asks of us, and subsequently falling short of His desires. It is amazing that thousands of us can go into a man-made organization like the military with assurance of our own career decisions and confident that the US taxpayers will supply our needs. Yet, we are anxious that our loving God will maroon us in an undesirable situation short on supplies and destined for failure. What does He promise, though? He promises to build us, equip us, and train us. And unlike a general giving us orders, He promises to lead us like a shepherd. He promises to prosper us amply that we might serve Him well and bring Him glory wherever He leads. He asks only that we first show our trust in Him.

It's quite an enlistment that God has placed before us—citizens of the kingdom. We don't have to be young to enlist, and we are never too old for the commitment. We don't have to enlist at all. We are eternally secure in the knowledge that we shall dwell in the house of the Lord forever. What could be better than that? I guess it's a matter of being all we were meant to be.

Onward…Christian Soldiers.

Stewart R. Shipp
Peachtree Corners

A Plan To Pray Like We Give

I've a friend who has never been thrilled with the idea of New Year's resolutions. This is especially true with resolutions about his prayer life. Every year he resolves to step up his prayer life. He wants to pray more and pray more effectively, but he just can't seem to do it, even though he sets fairly modest goals each year. All he wants to do is to pray for five minutes each day. He starts off so well, but according to his time records, he seems to be dreadfully behind schedule by late January. He is completely out of whack by summer with no way to catch up to his annual goal. He always feels guilty. He always feels foolish. After a while he begins to rationalize that there's no real standard requirement for prayer; nobody prays enough anyway, and there's always next year.

It occurred to him, though, that he is usually able to keep his annual stewardship commitment. He budgets a specific amount of money for the year, and by the end of the year he comes fairly close to giving his expectations. He feels good about it. He feels smart. So, this year he is resolving to pray like he gives. After all, five minutes per day amounts to only about 30 hours for the year. He can easily fit 30 hours of prayer into his year. Both prayer and giving really have so much in common. Each is worship. Each strengthens our trust in God. Each offers a spiritual relationship with God. So why not approach them with the same resolve? It's a two-for-one resolution.

This is his plan for prayer. As with his giving, he will attack the big numbers first and fill-in with the rest more spontaneously over the year. He can knock off a good portion of the prayer commitment in large portions of, say, three-hour chunks. He sees Easter Week, with Palm Sunday, Good Friday, and Easter Sunday, offering a good opportunity to pray a full three, maybe three-and-a-half hours—at least 10% of his commitment. There's the year end Christmas prayer time. Between the afternoon and evening Christmas Eve services, he can get another hour and a half. That's another five percent of the commitment there. Other opportunities may arise unexpectedly, like during a long airplane ride. Surely he can knock out half of his commitment with these big pushes.

To parallel his offering schedule, he may have to cut back daily prayers during the summer. Things come up you know. The kids are out of school. There's vacation. It's so hot. Who can pray during all that? He intends to do more praying when things are going very, very well—after all there's nothing like thanking God for your blessings. He doesn't like to think about it, but he will probably pray less when things are getting more difficult. Again, this is his pattern for giving, so why not for prayer?

During the worship service, he can skip the congregational prayers if he is ahead of his prayer budget. If others notice him not praying, he can give them the "I-usually-pray-on-the-first-of-the-month" shrug. All in all, he is assured that once he applies himself to this prayer commitment regimen, God will see a quality of prayer quite different from previous years.

He figures this arrangement will begin to reap benefits like his offering budget does. First, in December, Floy, the church treasurer, is sure to ask him if he intends to pray as much as he did last year. Floy's been good about financial shepherding, so surely he will be concerned about my friend's prayer commitment, too. Second, he'll begin to work out problems by himself, without having to lift these burdens to God. After all, his experiences with his finances have taught him to postpone giving to God during difficult times. Things generally work out, and he's eventually back on budget. Then the prayers can get back on pace. Furthermore, he'll eventually discover that he can get by without committing his entire prayer budget. At year's end, a total of 25 hours will begin to look pretty good; that's over two hours a month. He can leave it at that without interrupting the family's Christmas plans, without another five hours of prayer. Things will generally work out. He'll feel good about it.

Too whimsical? I hope my whimsy is instructive. Prayer is both our worship to God and our relationship with God. Likewise, our offerings are worship. Hence, we give our offerings during the worship service. Our offerings also define our relationship with God. In our giving, we acknowledge the many, many blessings that are gifts from God. Yet we are professing, even with these blessings, that we have anxieties and uncertainties about personal finances. Despite these concerns, our giving is a sign of our trust in God's steadfast faithfulness and, yes, even his promises for prosperity. Our trust should be unwavering. Shouldn't our giving at least be routine? Yes, there's a place for large, single monetary gifts to the church; just like there's a time for on-your-knees, extended prayer. But there is value in going to God in prayer often, even unceasingly. And so it is with regularly giving to God. Give regularly.

Trust in God. Now there's a good New Year's resolution.
Stewart R. Shipp
Peachtree Corners

I See They're Playing Golf. Can This Really Be Heaven?

This spring I'm going to take up the game of golf. When I see those TV promotions about the Masters Tournament, I want to be a golfer. Nowhere do spring and golf come together better than down the road at Augusta National. I should inform you that every spring for the past 15 years I've also taken up the game of golf, each time rather unsuccessfully. I usually begin to prepare for my spring golf during January. There's not much opportunity to play golf in January, so mostly I read about golf until I can put my newly learned techniques into play.

In my mind I've got a pretty expansive repertoire. I've read from the old-timers: Bobby Jones, Tommy Armour, and Sam Snead. I've read from the veteran players: Jack Nicklaus, Tom Watson, and Greg Norman. I've read from the current stars, the popular teaching pros and even a few caddies. I've read little red books, big green books, books with pictures, and books with diagrams. I've read about grips, stances, back-swings, straight elbows, heads-down, finishing high, whew…I've read a lot. Plus, I can assure you that every golfer in Peachtree Corners has at least one tip that has never failed him. I've heard at least a dozen different ways to get out of a greenside bunker, several ways to chip and run, knock it down, or flop it up. Some tips are new experiments; some are old standards. But, my best bet would be to stick with the guys who play at Augusta—the recognized masters.

Stewardship is a lot like golf. You can read a lot about stewardship, too. In the Bible, there seem to be an inexhaustible number of scriptures about giving, tithing, and managing financial resources. Here are some stewardship references that I have run across for you planning to boost your stewardship form this year. I encourage you to read the references and take them to heart. I think you'll find them to be a blessing.

- Give reverently   Deuteronomy 14:23
- Give to glorify God   2 Kings 4:42-44
- Give thankfully   2 Corinthians 12
- Give as a blessing to others   Acts 20:35
- Give routinely and methodically   1 Corinthians 16:2
- Give according to your ability   Mark 12:41-44
- Give expecting God's mercy   Luke 6:38
- Give voluntarily and cheerfully   2 Corinthians 9:6-7
- Give trusting God   Proverbs 11:28

Now, back to golf. After all that winter reading, I've eventually got to put the ball in play. Come May or June, I'll be on my favorite course's signature par-three hole. It's the 17th hole, a water hole with about a 155-yard carry to the front of the green. I'll have had a decent round so far, having lost maybe only three balls. As I step up to the tee, I'll begin to think about that big, huge pond separating my ball and the green. That day I'll be trying to focus on Greg Norman's tips about his grip, his stance, his swing, and his follow-through. Then I'll begin to remember Greg at Augusta National at Amen Corner on the par-three 12th hole teed up 155 yards from the hole. Through the years, Greg has had problems there. Personally, I can't forget watching his ball rise powerfully into the sky, and then drop disastrously into Rae's Creek in front of the green. So, I'll begin to think that maybe Greg isn't so wise; maybe his tips aren't so good. After all, he never won at Augusta. So, I look at the water and decide I need to make a few changes to suit my circumstances. I should change my stance a little, my grip some, and maybe my backswing. I should use that special way I lift my elbow in my follow through. This time I'll do it my way. After all, we have to play our own ball, don't we? Whish, Thud, Splash.

I don't know how you go about preparing your stewardship ministry. Just like in golf, reading about stewardship doesn't get you any closer to its blessings. But unlike golf, the stewardship scriptures are not tips; they are truth. They are reliable. They do not change from generation to generation. They are meant for everyone and are to be played on every course of life. They are from a single, eternal trustworthy source. Jesus himself lived these truths. In golf you've got to play your ball as it lies. In your own stewardship ministry, sooner or later you've got to put something into play, even if that means you do nothing and just pass the plate. You can follow your own particular way with your own expectations and with your own philosophy for giving. You can do whatever you feel is right for your special circumstances. Or, you can follow God's way. The outcomes are up for comparison.

I never even dream to play at Augusta National, but I long for us to meet on the Master's course. I hear it's beautiful.

Stewart R. Shipp
Peachtree Corners

O Lord! What Have You Done with the Amway Guy?

It's been said there is nothing like a powerful personal testimony for a strong stewardship campaign. I've been hopeful that I could interview some rich philanthropist for such impact. It would be great to interview some rich guy and find that he followed God's word to achieve his own prosperity. There are a couple of reasons I haven't graced these pages with such an interview. First, there's a simple matter of knowing a real rich guy. Sure, I know some rich folks, but for my first interview I want a really, really rich guy. My readers deserve nothing less. Right now, I'm not sure if I have a clear fix on the qualifying threshold of wealth. Second, I'm cautious that some of the really rich philanthropist may turn out to have feet of clay. I'm often suspicious that such conspicuous generosity to Christian ministries will someday be discovered as an outcome of rather disreputable ventures and only meant to balance the donor's sense of doing something good. Such an eventual revelation tends to destroy a considerable share of the intended impact for Christian stewardship. I don't want to fall into that trap.

To my delight, I read an article in the Wall Street Journal[1] that may be a good substitute for such an interview. It featured Richard DeVos, co-founder of Amway Corp. I guess I could simply have you read the article for yourself, but I wouldn't be earning my keep. So, let me paraphrase a few of the thoughts. First, Mr. DeVos is Christian, "a life-long member of the Christian Reformed denomination." As a Calvinist, he's one of us. He and his colleague formed Amway in 1959. Today, Forbes magazine estimates that Mr. DeVos is worth $3.4 billion. Now get this part: "When he was married (in 1953), his wife, Helen, informed him that they would be tithing their income,

---

[1] *Door-to-Door Faith*, by Arthur C. Brooks, Wall Street Journal, 4/21/06

according to biblical teaching, 10% to charity and no excuses." God bless you, Helen.

The article continues, "They have also always practiced the habit of giving 50% of their charity to explicitly Christian causes. Over the years the couple has donated nearly $400 million to charitable causes in health, education, the arts, public policy and—especially—religion." I've never had an opportunity to hear Mr. DeVos speak, but I'll bet he has a heart-warming testimony. Mr. DeVos customarily recites selected Proverbs as the promise of prosperity here on earth. The paper quotes him, "God blesses a generous heart; when you give, He makes the pot fuller."

I was very close to picking up the telephone and calling Mr. DeVos for an exclusive *Chimes* interview. Then it hit me. This Mr. Amway-Rich-Guy may not be all he is cracked up to be. You do the math. First, Mr. DeVos is worth $3.4 billion and he gave $400 million to charity, of which only 50% was for Christian causes. Second, you know he didn't save everything he's earned. Surely, he has splurged a little of his income somewhere along the line. So the numbers say that he didn't actually tithe. I've got him pegged at about 3-5% for Christian work. That's a far cry from the traditional tithing standards.

I haven't asked Floy, our church treasurer, but I'm guessing that here at Peachtree Corners we've never had a $200 million donor in our 170-year history, nor have we turned one down. I'm quite sure that if Mr. DeVos walked up to our door with a check in his hand, at least six deacons would have me bound in duct tape and stashed away in a broom closet before I could get the first accusatory charge out of my mouth. So much for *Chimes* investigative reporting.

So, I'm thinking that if a rich, compassionate, Christian gentleman like Richard DeVos can't follow God's rules about stewardship, how can I continue to remind a congregation about God' promises through tithing? Mr. DeVos has given hundreds of millions and has still fallen short. How can I urge the giving of mere thousands? I've got two responses. Neither may be right, but I bet they both are. First, giving is about God, not about mankind. We have a bountiful God. God is so bountiful in his promises that even billionaires can't keep up. Mr. DeVos talks about a "fuller pot." God desires to give him a *bigger pot*. We don't have the capacity to keep pace with all that God provides. We can't outgive the Giver. Glory be to God.

Second, I look back to a young married couple in 1953. Even to attempt to tithe then was a Herculean effort. Shortly after WWII and Korea, still six years before Amway was formed, and many years before the company gained stability, this young Christian couple trusted that God was in their future. If God promised it, they would trust it. I don't have the mind of God, but I'll surmise that those tithes then were more precious than all the millions to come. We have an eternal God. He desires that we live within Him. He never looks back and asks, "What have you done for me lately." Nor should we.

Stewart R. Shipp
Peachtree Corners

TITHING BY THE NUMBERS FOR *DUMMIES*

So exactly how much is a tithe? That seems to be a common question. The word itself means "one-tenth." But that was for Old Testament times. That was about goats, sheep and baskets of grain. Let's get down to dollars and cents. What does tithing mean in 21st century terms? This question is disrupting modern America. After all, we want to be seen as a nation giving our share to good causes.

> ⌘ Stewart Shipp's note: This article was written for a *Chimes* April issue. The *Chimes* editors don't receive many comments from the readers, but this was an exception. Several readers objected to the legalism proposed by the article. Many readers have told me that this article is nowhere near my usual high standards for journalistic excellence. Some said this article stinks. Yet, I stand resolute in my freedom of expression. My response to those critics is that this was written for the *Chimes* April issue. In a rather sophomoric frame of mind, I thought it would be funny to make an April Fools' comment. I thought I would structure it like the popular books for "Dummies." It's a joke! It's an April Fools' joke. Okay, usually great comedians don't have to explain their jokes. What can I say—I'm not a great comedian. So explanations seem to be necessary. I will add further commentary for the purpose of explaining my joke and my intentions.

This month I thought I would spend some time on a method to build your "tithe." I am convinced that many of us are more generous than we may realize. I believe that by using this methodology, you will soon be able to claim tithing levels never imagined. I expect that you will reach not only the traditionally accepted "10%" threshold, but will see your tithes reach 25%, 30% and more. Relying on this method, you will find that your self-esteem will improve incredibly.

> ⌘ **Stewart Shipp's note: I trust that I don't have to remind you that we don't give for self-esteem, but apparently I can't afford to be too subtle.**

We, of course, tithe from our income, but not every facet of our income is subject to tithing. Certainly experts would acknowledge that deferred compensation, contributions to pensions, and IRA's should be removed from our tithe-able income. If the government is willing to wait for these to become actual income, surely your church treasurer can do the same. If you own a home, I am convinced that the annual appreciation of your home should be included in tithe-able income. Any real estate broker would be glad to give you an estimate of your home's appreciated value, and you will be delighted with the bond of friendship that results from such requests. The appreciated value can be adjusted with the appropriate present value reasonable to current mortgage rates, and for a time period that you expect to remain in your home. Any banker will calculate this present value for you, and again, a relationship may become a long-lasting friendship. I believe the clearest and most biblical recognition of income is found in the 1992 IRS regulations. The treatment of dividends, municipal bond interest, and preferential capital gain fairly excludes these cash flow earnings from your tithe-able "earned" income. Fortunately, the Form 1040 for that year was rather straightforward, and I suggest that you use that format as a guide to determine your "Net Tithe-able Income."

> ⌘ Stewart Shipp's note: I thought the preceding paragraph was hilarious with the ironic comparison of Christian tithing to the IRS. Ostensibly, the US Government says that all citizens should pay taxes at a rate of 28%, a rather simple, straightforward concept. There are some exceptions to this general premise. To explain these exceptions in regulatory terms, the IRS issues a tax code that has over 2,300 pages, well over 2.5 million words. The IRS employs over 95,000 employees to explain, review and enforce the paying of this statutory rate of 28% (with exceptions). Frequently, the government reprints these regulations with substantial changes due to new tax legislation, prevailing tax court rulings, or edits by IRS folks who have decided that they didn't know what the doggone thing meant either.
>
> Furthermore, taxpayers are allowed 10 months after the tax year to finally calculate what their actual taxes are. I'm thankful that God doesn't work like the IRS. My personal Bible has 1,061 pages. I'm grateful that it doesn't have 3,361 pages with mostly mind-numbing language defining tithes. I'm grateful that God's word is eternal and doesn't have to be reissued every few decades as our economic parameters change.
>
> Are you beginning to pick up the article's humor? If not, maybe joking about the IRS tax forms just can't be funny to everyone.

The obvious place to look for your hidden tithes is your paycheck withholdings. Not all withholdings qualify as tithes, since not all are really for "good works." Certainly, Social Security deductions to help the retired and provide health insurance for the indigent are easily seen as benevolence. Don't forget to take credit for your employer's portion of the deduction, since biblically a corporation was not a tithing entity. The United Fund's Fair Share is purely charitable giving, as they advertise, therefore included as part of your tithe. Federal withholdings are a little tricky, but the 5% portion of the Federal budget allocated to Defense spending should not be considered a tithe, in my opinion. State taxes have no benevolent uses, I am told, and so these account for no tithes. Unemployment insurance is a helping hand to the jobless and is a worthy tithe. Group insurance will depend upon your own health, so subtract your actual medical and accident claims from your gross group insurance deductions to calculate your tithe. Political donations don't qualify as tithes, sorry.

> ⌘ **Stewart Shipp's note: I just couldn't help myself for writing this paragraph. It seems that many of us have come to see our government as the Supreme Being to answer all our problems and cure all our woes. The logical progression would be to think that any "donation" to the government is somehow holy was too much for me to overlook. This is worth a least a snicker from those less inclined to see the government as our guardian angel.**

Cash contributions, of course, are good tithing items. Gifts to colleges sponsoring progressive scientific research are tithes. Support for the athletic endeavors of those college researchers is an important component, too. I would suggest that contributions should be made to both Georgia and Georgia Tech to safely assure the full gamut of good works. Speaking of colleges, tuition payments for your children to attend Erskine College, our church supported school, can be included as tithes, as long as your child is not majoring in Business Administration—after all, tithing is intended to help mankind, not exploit it. Tickets bought for the symphony, theater, and puppetry workshops that go unused should be good for something, so consider them to be tithes.

> ⌘ Stewart Shipp's note: This paragraph was meant to parody some of the thoughts of sincere people with good intentions but a misunderstanding of Christian stewardship. Their reasoning is that God wants us to "do good," therefore anything that goes for "doing good" must be favorable to God. Don't get me wrong. In general, organizations chartered to "do good" do just that…they "do good" for mankind, whether in science, health, education, or the common weal. I believe this type of giving may be what Paul was referring to as a gift of the Holy Spirit (1 Cor. 13:3). All believers are encouraged to give for the reasons I've covered. A few have the special gift for giving beyond the tithes to the poor, as Paul cites, or to the deserving, whatever good organization that is.
>
> The fallacy in counting these donations as part of your tithing discipline is found in a couple of concerning areas. First, we deem our donations as going toward good. I'm sure that few, if any, of our expenditures are meant to be toward "bad." So, we have a fuzzy definition of just what is for "good," when almost everything we do is for "good." Second,

> yet foremost: how do these donations bring glory to God without the worship or service facets of Christian stewardship? If they don't, I'm hard pressed to see them as part of our Christian tithe.
>
> As you can see, I've woven these fallacies into my article quite adeptly, ready to spring the trap shut on the unsuspecting reader. It's a literary practical joke that I've set up. This is really a funny article.

You can now determine precisely your real tithing percentage. Once you have reached 10% there's no holding back. Soon, even 20-30% seems so close. You just have to look for it. You just feel so...so...meaningful. There's no feeling quite like being with friends and tossing out, "Yep, I tithe 35% to my good causes." Makes you feel good to be a thirty-five percenter, doesn't it?

> ⌘ Stewart Shipp's note: With today's ease of financial record keeping, along with our decimal based monetary system, it's so easy to make a ratio of anything to anything. Some of these ratios come under the heading of "So What?" I'm trying to let the reader see that feeling good because of a contrived ratio is a non-starter. Ten percent is a ratio, not a doctrine.

I should point out that only the Old Testament speaks to tithing; the New Testament doesn't mention it at all. That's not to say that tithing to God became unimportant sometime after Malachi but before Matthew. Giving consistently, giving generously, and giving worshipfully are encouraged throughout Paul's letters. Jesus teaches the blessing of "loving the Lord your God with all your heart and with all your soul and with all your mind" (Matt. 22:37). If I'm not mistaken, "all" means 100%. Christ wants us to be a one hundred percenter. If you're into percentages, toss that one out to your "thirty-five-percent" friends. How does that make you feel?

> ⌘ Stewart Shipp's note: Even with our best efforts to quantify so much of our life, sometimes it's just impossible. For example, many of us are concerned about our weight. Some of us are overweight, and one or two of us are underweight. To regulate our weight we sometimes look to our daily intake of calories. Assume that you are intending to consume 1,800 calories per day. Do you know exactly how many calories you consumed today, yesterday, or last Thursday? Did you eat one additional celery stick to get you dead-on your 1,800 calories target? Obviously you didn't. But, I'll bet that you did know when you hadn't eaten enough or when you had stuffed yourself. Sometimes you know you should eat more and other times less. Tithing is a lot like that. Unfortunately, the strict definition is "10%." That's a good target, but it's not an exact science. It's a target that is attainable, but large enough to make you put forth an effort to achieve it. It makes you aware of your relationship with God and demonstrates to you that you must trust in God as you tithe. You are not required, nor are you encouraged, to do better than 10%. But sometimes you wind up doing less than you think you should have; other times you actually do more than you thought you could. All in all, it appears that God set a pretty logical target. In giving our 10% by whatever method we calculate it, we are closer to trusting our Lord 100%. That's the real percentage He desires.

> This note had nothing to do with the April Fools' joke, but the thought occurred to me as I was writing the article: Even April Fools' jokes can provoke deep thought.

⌘ Stewart Shipp's note: So, did you finally get it? Did you see how I linked the legalism of the IRS returns due on April 15th and the foolishness of April Fools' Day into a message about legalistic attitudes and foolish ways often infused into Christian stewardship? You say you don't get it? I mean, "April Fool!" It's a traditional day for joking. Well…er…never mind…I guess you had to be there. Goodness, the month of May can't get here soon enough.

Enjoy your April, both the 15th and the 1st.
Stewart R. Shipp
Peachtree Corners

Chapter Four

PROSPERITY

God promises prosperity for those who give. That's worth repeating: God promises prosperity.

> One man gives freely, yet gains even more; another withholds unduly, but comes to poverty. A generous man will prosper; he who refreshes others will himself be refreshed.
> (Prov. 11:24,25)

God promises prosperity. I don't fully know what this means. Granted, the gift of our eternal life is more prosperity than we deserve. For believers, eternal prosperity is guaranteed and not contingently promised to us as a result of our giving or tithing. I'm expecting that the promised prosperity is earthly, tangible and measurable. I believe God wants us to accept this prosperity and not to shun it. I'll surmise that God's prosperity plan is different for each of us. Yet, if God has planned it, it's beyond our imagination. It's beyond my understanding. I'm convinced that the prosperity planned for each of us will result in God's glory.

God's Prosperity Promises Are About Him, Not You

We know that trusting in God is the right thing to do.[1] But on the other hand, it must be wrong to trust God's promises of prosperity. I'm assuming that something is wrong because sincere, mature Christians seem to be so reluctant to talk about prosperity as a fruit of Christianity. On the rare occasion when main line Christians talk about it, it is in soft terms, with caution never to broach the nefarious territory of the Prosperity Doctrine Prophets.

It should be so simple to accept. God promises prosperity to those who trust Him and commit to him according to their means. There are many scripture verses that say this. In fact, there are too many to ignore or try to interpret otherwise. However, sincere, mature believers approach this simple proclamation with suspicion. The whole premise smacks of the TV evangelist pleading for money on the promise that God will multiply offerings so as to make rich folks out of all donors. God is contorted into a personal wealth machine. All we have to do is put one dollar in one slot and collect ten dollars from another slot. Prudent believers flee from such an idea. Surely our God of Love and Righteousness is of better mettle.

It is popular to construe that prosperity promises are not in terms that we mortals value, but in heavenly values. After all, the Lord has given us eternal life. What kind of prosperity can ever top that? To think in terms of hard assets, in terms of treasures, is mere greed and a distortion of the nature of God. Perhaps God's promises are more spiritual values like world peace, friendship, happiness, and such. They are promises of valuable things for us, but not necessarily bankable things. Yet, the scriptures

---

[1] Stewart Shipp bases this chapter on a stewardship committee report to the church elders and a separate Chimes message.

with promises of prosperity can't be edited away. They seem so straightforward, so emphatic, so convincing. Malachi says,

> "Bring the whole tithe into the storehouse, that there may be food in my house. Test me in this," says the Lord Almighty, "and see if I will not open the floodgates of heaven and pour out so much blessing that you will not have room enough for it. I will prevent pests from devouring your crops, and the vines in your fields will not cast their fruit," says the Lord Almighty. "Then all the nations will call you blessed, for yours will be a delightful land," says the Lord Almighty.
> (Mal. 3:10-12)

Upon reading this, even a sincere believer is prone to believe that God is referring to crops and land and bankable things—not just promising a delightful land in the hereafter. Prosperity is what God promises, but that's not what even our own casual observations show us. If this promise be true, why aren't all Christian rich? Sure, there are some very affluent Christians. There are some who are downright rich. But when we look into their riches, they have gained their stature very much like many non-believers. They inherited their wealth, or they were fortunate enough to be at the right place at the right time, or through persistent hard work they gradually accumulated their riches. They are certainly blessed, and most confess such. Yet, their fortunes are not so different than other rich folks that had no idea of God's promises. For most of us, the floodgates of heaven don't show any sign of opening. We've read the promises, and, yes, we are blessed in more ways than we can count. We know so many non-believers just like us who are also blessed, but, we suspect, have never given to the Lord in accordance with our own standards. So, we believe our own eyes. We won't admit to contradicting God's word, but we will shape it to our own observations. So, our best defense is to simply choose another part of the Bible to dwell on and ignore any thoughts of God's promised prosperity.

God has a pretty clever system here. In so many words He promises us prosperity. If we don't take Him up on the deal, then our lack of trust has diminished his promise. If we believe His promise, we will surely receive His blessings, but we risk finding out that His promise really was for world peace, and we are no better off than any of our fellow believers. We were chumps. We would have done just as well buying that new plasma TV instead of tithing.

Tell me that something else is going on. I think there is. I must say that this just doesn't sound like the Righteous and Loving God I know. If you are in anyway reluctant to embrace God's promises, I suggest we look at this in a different light. We may be missing something that could possibly change our entire relationship with the Lord.

Let's go back to one of the first promises of prosperity that the Lord gives to his children. As long ago as Abraham, God promised his children land—the Promised Land. Land was the quintessential indicator of prosperity. That same promise was repeated time and time again. Moses led his people out of Egypt for this promise. Millions of Israelites trusted God—even while wandering through the desert for forty years. Upon the eve of entry to the Promised Land, the Lord spoke to Joshua once again.

> After the death of Moses, the servant of the Lord, the Lord said to Joshua son of Nun, Moses' aide: "Moses my servant is dead. Now then, you and all these people, get ready to cross the Jordan River into the land I am about to give to them-to the Israelites. I will give you every place where you set your foot, as I promised Moses. Your territory will extend from the desert to Lebanon, and from the great river, the Euphrates–all the Hittite country–to the Great Sea on the

west. No one will be able to stand up against you all the days of your life. As I was with Moses, so I will be with you; I will never leave you nor forsake you."

(Josh. 1:1-5)

According to this, the Promised Land included a vast part of the then known world. It stretched from the southern desert to Lebanon in the north, from the Euphrates River in the east to the great Mediterranean Sea in the west. In today's terms, it included Saudi Arabia in the south, Lebanon and Syria in the north, Iraq and Kuwait in the east and Jordan with the east coast of the Mediterranean in the west. What an inheritance awaited the children of Israel. What a fortune was there before them. God had not forsaken them after their wanderings. God would not forsake them ever. His land was now their land, with no obstacles before them.

It seems that the Lord was big in promises, but small on delivery. Israel never reached the boundaries prescribed by God. The biblical Israel is much like the Israel of today. It was a small nation confined to a narrow sliver of land situated around the small Jordan River—a river of little economic and no geopolitical significance. The Israelites never expanded their land even to the nearby seacoast controlled by the Philistines. They never marched against the Hittites to the Euphrates. They never ventured into the neighboring Arabian Desert, then seemingly so desolate. Even today, the Jews have limited their Promised Land to that 8,000 square mile area.

It is as though the Lord handed the Israelites a large canvas—canvas with the paint-by-numbers all stenciled in. My grandson got a similar paint set last Christmas. I remember that by Christmas night he had already begun to paint the picture promised on the box cover of the set. The picture was never completed. There are only a few bright colors in the lower left corner of the paint board. Other Christmas gifts offered far more fun and entertainment. He was content in the fact that someday he could come back and complete the painting. But he never has. Now, to see my grandson's intended painting, I have to look at the promised picture on the box top.

In the biblical Israel we do not see a completed picture of the Promised Land, only a few strokes of paint in the far left corner, much like my grandson's project. It is only with hindsight that we can fill in the stenciled, unpainted picture. What a lovely picture the Lord had planned. Oh, it would have been so easy for the Lord to give Joshua an idea of what the final picture would have looked like. It would have been so easy to have a box top with the colors all filled in. With 21st century hindsight, perhaps I could insert a few verses into the book of Joshua. It's too late for Joshua, too late for Israel, but maybe it serves a purpose for us.

Joshua 1:5 and the next few verses may have been written like this:

> And the Lord then spoke to Joshua and the Israelite leaders. Set your feet over this Promised Land, from the Great Sea on the west and to the Euphrates River at your east, from the southern desert to the northern land of Lebanon, and I will grant you great prosperity. With the forests of Lebanon you will build great cities throughout the land. You will build a mighty navy to rule the seas; your bountiful shipping trade shall take you to all parts of the world. The Euphrates on your east will open to you the oceans to India, China, and Japan. Those nations will trade with you silk, tea, and precious gems. Your riches will abound, and you will proper as I have promised. The Great Sea on your west will open to you the lands of Europe, and even new worlds beyond the Great Sea bearing amber waves of grain. Yea, even Egypt, the land of your bondage, will bow to the power that the Lord God has given to you. In time this land will yield great resources of oil to propel your chariots and ships, and even

to fly among the clouds. As I have promised, the children of Israel shall prosper. O my Children, set your feet throughout the land. No one will stand against you.

Your prosperity and power will bring a great peace throughout the world, as all the nations will abide under the laws given to Moses by the Lord your God. The great peace shall stretch to the far corners of your sphere of power...to China, Japan, India, Egypt, Africa, and to the New World. This peace shall be called the time of *Shalom Israel*, and it shall last for thousands of years. My promised prosperity shall come to you and yea even to the people unto the far ends of the world. It shall begin by simply your treading the land that I laid forth before you. O my Children set your feet throughout the land. No one will stand up against you. Thus, the Israelites will be honored and revered as God Almighty's servants prospering in the promise of the Lord, your God.

And lo, I shall bring you a great and unimaginable prosperity—far exceeding the bounty in your vast treasury. For the Glory, Power, and Authority of the Lord your God, on the peak of the mountain of Abraham's sacrifice you will build a magnificent tabernacle, in the fashion I described to Moses. I shall send my only begotten Son to live among you. The Levites, anointed tabernacle priests, shall take my Son, the pure Lamb of God, to the Holy of Holy, to the Altar that you carried with you in the desert, to be sacrificed. His precious blood shall be shed for your lasting atonement and the redemption of your sins. He shall then become your tabernacle. The sins of the entire world will be forever forgiven, and peace will continue over the world that I so dearly love, until my Son returns again. Glory be to the Son.

It would have been great if God had given Joshua a hint of things to come. Yet even with such a God-given picture, I'm afraid Joshua and the children of Israel would not have done any differently than history tells us. The subsequent unwritten verses would continue:

> And thus it came to pass that Joshua and the leaders of the Israelites cast their eyes on the Mount called Zion, upon the Sea called Galilee, and upon the River Jordan and said among each other, "Thanks be to God for these blessings of the mountain, the sea, and the river in this land of milk and honey. We are blessed far beyond our sufferings as slaves in Egypt. We have wandered for 40 years in the desert, losing our fathers and our father's fathers. Our people are tired and unprepared for further walking. Were we to travel to the corners of the land laid forth before us by the Almighty God, is there any assurance that we can return to this beautiful mountain? Lord God, we worship you, we adore you, we honor you for all the days of our lives, yet we shall not seek more than what we have now and shall not tread another step. Save your blessings of prosperity, Lord. Your promises of prosperity were all about us we know; let us glorify you just as we are today. We don't need any more of your bountiful blessings. Empowered by you, we will strive to do great things from this small piece of land. O Lord, it's not about us. Let our work be about You.

> And so it came to pass that the Israelites stayed in the land of Canaan. None of the great deeds of the Lord were heard by the peoples throughout the once Promised Land. The power of the Lord was not seen throughout the Great Sea or from the oceans touching the Euphrates River. The land of China came under the authority of Buddha and Confucius and did not know the Lord God Almighty. The land of India embraced Hinduism and Zoroastrianism and did not know the Lord God Almighty. The Europeans became tribal polytheists and did not know the one true Lord. Lo, the land of the Euphrates was prepared for the coming of the false prophet of Mecca. Throughout the world, the darkness of evil reached farther than the light of the Lord of Israel.

And thus it came to pass that the Son of God did come to the world as God had foretold. He was born into the land taken by the men of Joshua. Sadly, there was no prosperity in the land—only a weak, backward, enslaved nation. It came to pass that the Son of God was led by foreign soldiers to be persecuted and beaten and crucified on a cross of the pagans. God's plan for atonement was all about His children, but it was performed on a stage far from the intended promise. The sacrifice of the Son was not seen by the world as glory, but as folly. The great promise was fulfilled not on a stage of prosperity, but of depravity.

Alas, it was now too late to complete the picture of the Promised Land. Today, we read the timeless promises of the Lord written in the Bible. Promises of prosperity continue for us. These promises are to each of those who have entrusted their bounty into the hands of the Lord. The Lord will give prosperity to them. This prosperity will be pleasing for them, even delightful. Yet even more, we are to reach out for these promises, not only for our delight, but also for the glory of God.

And the Lord God then appeared to the Christians members of churches across America. "O dear children, read my word. I have promised you prosperity if you will only trust in the Lord your God and relinquish a portion of the things that I have given to you first and return them to me in accordance with my word." The people of that blessed church in Peachtree Corners, looked at one another. "O God, O God, we wish to do so much more for you. We look at our building, we look at our work for you, and we look at our personal lifestyles and that of our country, our community, and our congregations. We enjoy a prosperity never imagined by our grandfathers. We drive our big new cars, live in big houses, have our retirement taken care of, and enjoy leisure never imagined by our fathers. O God, you have already blessed us with prosperity beyond that which we deserve. We don't need any more of your promises. This is enough for us, and besides it shouldn't be about us; it should be about you. So this is what we are going to do…"

I fear to continue the passage. I fear it's too easy to ignore God's continued promised and settle for his past blessings. It's not too late to complete the picture promised to us, whatever that may be. God's plans are not complete. The numbers are ready to be filled in.
Stewart R. Shipp
Peachtree Corners

Everybody Has a Buddy

I've known Buddy all my life. Believe me, you don't want to get Buddy started on Evolution. He's not a scientist, although he once wanted to be. Somewhere back in his formative years, he got diverted to a business career. He is now a businessman. However, he has a high appreciation for the orderly elegance of science. From the tiny microcosm of the chemical element to the vast cosmic universe, Buddy sees this orderliness as the work of God's creative hand. It's not only Intelligent Design, but it's Loving and Righteous Design. There is no other explanation for him. Not randomness, not evolution, not natural selection. God created all, and all was good, orderly and elegant from the get-go. The Bible says so, and Buddy sees it with his own eyes and believes it whole-heartedly. Buddy blames the schools for not teaching this.

A while back, when Buddy and I were at Bible study, I ran across a passage from Proverbs that I found interesting. Based upon his business background, I thought it might interest him, too.

> Trust in the Lord with all your heart and lean not on your own understanding. Honor the Lord with your wealth with the first fruits of all your crops; then your barns will be filled to overflowing, and your vats will brim over with new wine
> (Prov. 3:5, 9-10)

Well, Buddy exploded. He claimed this was the craziest financial advice imaginable. In a blathering rant he protested that accumulating wealth was not so easy. Furthermore, God had answered his prayers by sending him to business schools and by preparing him for tests and getting him through his career. "With God's help, I made it through. Was all that 'understanding' worth nothing?" he lamented. "This proverb has no consideration for internal rates of return, discounted cash flow, investment theory, or financial analysis. After all that help learning these things, does God now expect me to ignore all those important 'understandings'?"

"Buddy, Buddy," I interrupted. "All that understanding is important to have under you belt, but God is saying don't lean on that. Use it certainly, but don't lean on it. Trust God. He created all things so that we can use them for His glory. Whatever you have received as your wealth so far, lift it up first to the Lord. Glorify Him with it, and it says here that He promises full barns and brimming vats of it in return."

"Preposterous!" Buddy exclaimed. "Sure, God has a place in business, and I pray to Him a lot at work. Like during my company's negotiations with that French outfit when we couldn't reach agreement on equivalent contributions for the pending joint venture. I prayed for a solution to this impasse. Luckily, I remembered an old international business course just in time. Or, when I lost that big contract, but went ahead with my commitment to the church without a dime in my bank account. Fortunately, I was rescued by that regional manufacturing deal coming through in the nick of time. That was business, pure and simple. It's what you know that counts. Don't give me this crops-in-the-barn mumbo-jumbo. If that were true, why don't they teach it in schools?"

Buddy and I are still real close and I reckon we always will be. But sometimes I see that Buddy is a little inconsistent. The scientific side of Buddy believes God created the universe with all its scientific grandeur. Buddy is assured that this is true because the Bible says so, and he has a little bit of scientific understanding to affirm it. Yet, when it comes to personal finances, Buddy doesn't think the Lord gets much involved, even though the

Bible says He does. The financial Buddy just can't bring himself to trust the Lord's word completely, even when he can see a little bit of its fruits. That's just Buddy. Somewhere along the way, Buddy should have been taught this. I'm thinking that we should blame the schools. Pray for Buddy and me.

Stewart R. Shipp
Peachtree Corners

Giving Thanks First

Once again we celebrate the Pilgrims' first Thanksgiving. Sometimes we get the idea that the story begins and ends with the Pilgrims thanking God for providing them with enough food, even extra food, for a feast. Actually, it wasn't their first thanksgiving. After all, they were Christians, and a rather righteous group of Christians at that. It's quite likely that they gave thanks rather frequently. Also, it wasn't as if they came to the New World seeking bounteous harvests simply to throw a party. This was a pilgrimage to settle into a land where they could praise and thank God without persecution.

I'll surmise that when the long ocean journey concluded on Plymouth Rock, they also offered a sincere thanksgiving—maybe even kissed the ground. The winter was brutal. I've endured two winters in Massachusetts, and I can't imagine enduring a 17th century blizzard without central heating. But they did, and they thanked God afterwards. Again, the coming of springtime offered them hope that God would provide fertile soil and climate for their sustenance. And He did…apparently beyond their expectations.

Lately, when I read about their great Thanksgiving feast described by secular media, I am influenced to conclude that these Pilgrims were contestants on the reality show, "Survivor: Plymouth Rock." After a year of learning about the agricultural quirks of their new environment, they then could celebrate by thanking God for being battle-hardened and ready to be on their own. This, we have been led to conclude, was the beginning of traditional American self-reliance. "Thanks, God, your help meant a lot to us. There's no need to fret over us anymore. We can manage things by ourselves from here." It would be easy for them to say so. After all, they were where they wanted to be, doing what they wanted to do, with more resources than they had ever imagined. What great opportunities would have been lost if those Pilgrims had not continued their journey trusting in God. The very foundations of our great nation reach back into that community of faithful and trusting Christians. God was still leading them in their journey.

Their Thanksgiving was an event of worship. Yes, they were "giving" to God, but even more, they were relinquishing to God a certain portion of their harvest as a show of faith, trusting God, not their harvest. Now, some of us may relish eating a week's portion of food as an act of worship, but that's not quite what I mean. Other harsh winters were soon to follow, and they expected it. The prudent thing to do would have been to store the extra food away. These folks celebrated with the good food that they might need later. They trusted God, not their bounty. And we know that God had more bounty in store for them, and eventually for their descendants, our fellow citizens today. Those Christian Pilgrims trusted in God for their prosperity. They looked hopefully for a safe place to worship, which would have been bountiful enough. Our great nation arising from their faith was God's plan of prosperity.

Today, I see many folks celebrating and thanking God for their bounty, and they should. I see young graduates thanking God for a good education. It would be so easy for them to say, "Thanks for everything I've learned, God. I'll take it from here." I see young careerists, finishing a lucrative project, thanking God for what this means to the family. It would be easy to say, "Thanks for everything I've earned, God. I'll take it from here." I see prosperous executives thanking God for organizations that do so much for so many. It would be so easy say, "Thanks for everything I've built, God. I'll take it from here." I see retirees, thanking God for the foresight to plan for retirement. It would be easy to say, "Thanks for everything I've saved, God. I'll take it from here." What missed opportunities! God has so much more in store for each and every one of us. He is assuredly pleased with our thanksgiving, but is yearning for our continued trust…our trust in Him, not trust in our bounty.

As we gather around our Thanksgiving tables, we will thank God for his blessings. In our thanksgiving, let's think in terms of showing trust in God's promises of the bountiful blessings in store for us. Let's give with thanks and also give with trust.

Happy Trust-giving,
Stewart R. Shipp
Peachtree Corners

TEN MILLION DOLLARS PLEDGED TO LOCAL CHURCH

Recently I had the privilege of witnessing a young man pledge $10,000,000 to a local church. The event was not covered by the press and was generally overlooked by the community. Surprisingly, those in attendance were not as impressed with the commitment to the extent that I was. On the other hand, even the donor was not the least bit dismayed at the lack of publicity accompanying his generosity. The fellow made this pledge at a nearby Texaco convenience store. While he was waiting in line to buy a $100,000,000 lottery ticket, I overheard him whispering to his pal that he intended to tithe his winnings to a local church. I made the ten million dollar calculation in my head. Bless his heart. I don't know whether or not the young donor was currently tithing; I suspect not.

I'm reminded of Jesus' parable about the Master's gift of talents. You remember the story (if not, it is found in Matthew 25:14-30). Before going on a trip the Master gives his servants one talent, two talents, or five talents. The more gifted servants put their money to work for the Master. Obviously, everyone in their town knew of their displayed gifts. The least gifted servant hides his one talent. No one in the town could possibly know of his gift. Upon the Master's return, the one-talent servant is rebuked and thrashed. I've never liked this parable. On the face of it, thrashing seems overly harsh. Furthermore, every time I hear this parable I feel like I may be headed for a horsewhipping. Why does Jesus pick on the poor one-talent fellow? Surely there are two-talent people who also hide their gifts, what happens to them? Why can't there be a lesson in here for those five-talent show-offs, too?

Jesus' wisdom endures for centuries. Once upon a time, Jesus must have told this parable for me to hear personally two thousand years later. Too often I feel like that one-talent servant, not quite confident enough, not quite trusting enough, to "invest" what I should for the Lord. I hold out for a few more talents, hiding from the world what I already have. Intuitively, I surmise that each of us occasionally considers himself to be that one-talent character. Look at our plight. We budget to the last penny with little to spare. We would be a lot more generous and do a lot more if we only had five times, or even twice, as much as we have now. I guess I've thought a thousand times about what I would give to the Lord if I had a financial windfall. I could give so much more. If I could land that big commission, or bonus, or reward, then I would endow a church building program. "Just wait, Lord, your big payoff is coming. Maybe next year. I may even take a shot at this week's lottery. You may have given me only one talent so far, Lord, but someday I'll earn my five talents for you, so help me God…so help me, God. Won't you please help me?"

I do deserve a good old-fashioned thrashing. I'm just another neighbor in Peachtree Corners, more than likely in the same situation as you. Yet, I dare say 95% of the world would trade places with me, straight up. In the eyes of the world I do have five talents. But let's not stop there. I'll say that half of America dreams to be where I am. So, to half of my neighbors I have at least two talents to their one. The world is wondering, just how much am I waiting for before I invest my talents the Lord has given me?

Each of us is a materially gifted, multi-talented servant. But material riches are not what the parable is about. While we have our material blessings, these are not the really valuable talents given to us by the Master. Jesus has given us eternal life. Nothing has twice, or even five times, the value of enjoying eternal life in the presence of our Lord. Jesus believed that to be very valuable. He died for it. Jesus sees us as His five-talent servants.

Even so, Jesus understood that his five-talent children often hear His parable with one-talent ears.

Rather than waiting for some lucky payoff, I should be living, serving, and showing the world the blessed assurance of this immeasurable gift. No matter how I feel about myself, in the eyes of my Master I'm a five-talent servant. Upon his return, he would be pleased if I had acted like it.

"Everyone who has will be given more, and he will have an abundance" (Matt. 25:29).

Stewart R. Shipp
Peachtree Corners

Practical Stewart Shipp Advice with a Divine Return

I've tried to keep these articles on a spiritual level explaining Christian stewardship as a means of worship, extolling the fruits of the church's service through stewardship, and suggesting that tithing is a Christian discipline we should all strive to attain and then maintain. Yet, I've heard that some of you are looking for Stewart Shipp's practical advice. You have some good questions. What's the best way to handle your credit card debt? How much mortgage should you take on? Should you lease, finance or pay cash for a car? How do you get out of debt? Your personal finances are in shambles, so what can you do to straighten them out?

For your sake I'll finally try to give you some easily understood and very practical advice. First, I ask you to read the following passage from Amos. Then, read it twice more.

> "I gave you empty stomachs in every city and lack of bread in every town yet you have not returned to me," declares the Lord. "I also withheld rain from you when the harvest was still three months away. I sent rain on one town, but withheld it from another. One field had rain; another had none and dried up. People staggered from town to town for water but did not get enough to drink, yet you have not returned to me," declares the Lord. "Many times I struck your gardens and vineyards, I struck them with blight and mildew. Locusts devoured your fig and olive trees, yet you have not returned to me," declares the Lord.
>
> (Amos 4:6-9)

Around 750 b.c. Israel was an agricultural society. Famines, poor harvests, parched lands, mildew and locust were plights of those long ago farmers. According to Amos, the Lord even takes credit for causing these miserable circumstances; it's like He let awful things happen to them just to get their attention. I'm sure that they longed for some good practical advice to overcome these miseries. Thank the Lord, with agricultural advancements and modern distribution methods we don't have to deal with these misfortunes as much as those folks did.

These days we have to deal with a curse that may be even more debilitating. In the United States this curse affects a substantial number of households. It now is greater than it has ever been in the history of our country. Today, we must deal with personal debt.

It's very likely that you have some personal debt. Credit cards, car loans and home mortgages have allowed us benefits otherwise unattainable. I have friends who are bankers; they reckon that their loan activity is a service, not a curse. In fact, they are right. Debt has accelerated our national economic growth and prosperity immensely over the past century. Maybe debt has been a useful tool for you and is not overbearing. But, for more than a few, debt is a crushing force. It shifts our focus from the Lord to our own desperate situation, and the Lord is not glorified as He desires. Overwhelming debt is 180 degrees contrary to the Lord's prosperity promises. The Lord desires us to glorify Him and enjoy His promises of prosperity. Clearly, He doesn't want us to be overwhelmed with debt.

So here is my practical advice. Read Amos 4:6-9 again. Now I know that there's a lot of advice out there that's a little more complicated. Some advice may involve personal budgets, loan consolidations, tax savings, additional jobs, and whatever else. If we are not smart enough to tackle these complicated measures, then we may want to consult a really, really smart financial advisor or enroll in an evening personal finance course to set a course to get ourselves out of this predicament. Or we can simply read Amos 4:6-9 again and again, until we understand God's message. Could it be that God is declaring, "I burdened you with overwhelming credit card balances, yet you have not returned to me"? It's like He is trying to get our attention.

You say: "Stewart Shipp, it can't be so simple." Well, we all know that we can't out-smart God. This passage lets us know that we can't be too stupid for God either. God has our personal answer, no matter what our expertise is. His solution is a whole lot better than any advice I could dream up. If God promises to halt a swarm of locusts merely if Israelite farmers return to him, what chance does our debt have?

Return to Him. Return to Him with prayer, with praise, and with trust. Your trust is your relinquishing to Him the substance of your misery. I advise you to lift up your personal finances to the Lord. God promises prosperity; I can't accept that He desires our languishing in personal debt. Start trusting God with a disciplined offering commitment. At first, it may be hard to give much at all, but it gets easier as your finances become manageable and tithing becomes a part of your life. I don't know how or when the Lord will repair your finances, or where the Lord will lead you. I do believe that He will do both in accordance with His plan.

Prosperity may come in steps. Each step may be as refreshing as rain to the farmers of Israel, or the removal of blight from their fields, or the filling of their empty stomachs. I've heard many testimonies about financial miracles that turn imminent disasters around in the nick of time. I'm not sure they were miracles, but fulfilled promises.

Stewart R. Shipp
Peachtree Corners

About the Authors

Stewart R. Shipp: The Real Skinny

Okay, so you've read some, if not all, of my messages. I'll go ahead and state the obvious. There is no Steward R. Shipp. Quite frankly, I'm not sure there ever could be. I've wanted to write such articles for a long time, but the task seems so daunting. Maybe the cover of the *nom de plume* helped prod me to the word processor. I've found it's a bold person, indeed who can say, "Look at me. I'm the expert on Christian stewardship. I'm prosperous. I'm talented. I've accumulated enough 'points' to appoint myself as a spokesperson for giving to God." Who could confidently hold their personal worship as exemplary for others to follow? I would rather not have my finances audited to grade my stewardship discipline. On the other hand, across the globe and throughout history there are thousands of Stewart Shipps. There are too many Stewart Shipps for any one of them to stand up, even humbly, as being the only one. Christians all over the world, throughout the ages, have been blessed to experience the power of giving and stewardship far more than this writer has ever imagined. So let's make a deal. If you will seek to become a true "Stewart R. Shipp," I promise that I'll also try. With God's help, we both can be:

Stewart R. Shipp

STEWART R. SHIPP AND ME

First, thanks for reading this far, or for skipping over to see who would attempt to write a book on Christian stewardship. As you probably know, books about Christian stewardship are usually written by Christian leaders with extensive theological backgrounds. I'm neither a preacher nor a theologian. Otherwise, these books are written by wealthy individuals who have overcome some degree of indigence, then had a meaningful epiphany with the Lord, and are now living happily ever after. I'm not rich. Every now and then, a popular journalist will write or edit such a book relying on the credibility of his reputation to attract interest in such a mundane subject. This is the first book that I've ever written. Occasionally, some wacky raconteur hopes to enliven the drudgery of stewardship by using a gregarious spin to spice up otherwise bland anecdotes. Not me, I'm Presbyterian. But, "I can do everything through him who gives me strength" (Phil. 4:13).

For a long time, I used Paul's message to the Philippians as a personal credo. I suppose that's good. I liked the idea that "I can do everything." I had big dreams and ambitions. I figured the Lord would give me the strength to accomplish these big dreams and satisfy a big ambition. I wanted to accomplish these dreams in the business world. I had the faith that strength would come from my preparation, and I asked God to prepare me for my dreams.

I prepared. Frankly, I prepared well. I have a bachelor's degree in economics from the University of Tennessee, an MBA from Harvard Business School, a Georgia CPA certificate, and a career in corporate accounting and finance in Atlanta. With a background like that, a person should have all the financial answers for prosperity and wise financial management. I'd like to be able to pass them along to you in this book, but between you and me, the financial answers learned at business schools or in the business world are not the answers for true and lasting prosperity. The elements of business administration have little to do with joy, and they hardly make for a deep relationship with God. Christian stewardship bears the fruits of prosperity, but it is not only about prosperity.

Along the way, the big dreams adjusted and the big ambition changed. What didn't fade was Paul's message. It's just that I better realized what it said…from its beginning.

> I have learned to be content whatever the circumstances. I know what it is to be in need, and I know what it is to have plenty. I have learned the secret of being content in any and every situation, whether well fed or hungry, whether living in plenty or in want. I can do everything through him who gives me strength.
>
> (Phil. 4:11-13)

I indeed have had plenty, and I know what it is to be in need. I was once Chief Financial Officer for a company that went public. I've enjoyed some big-time capital gains. I have had other business experiences that have not had outcomes so pleasant. But the Lord continued, and still continues, to provide me my daily bread. I am content, but I still have dreams. I dream that I can serve and glorify God as He has prepared me. I pray that I have served God when I had plenty, and I trust that I have served Him when I was in need. I have served in both times, according to the strength that God gave me. I can be needy, but not in need. God knows that I can do everything that He desires me to do in my neediness. I can have plenty, if plenty is needed to do all the things God desires me to do. Paul was content during his ups and downs. Truthfully, I am excited because I believe God's plans are much bigger than my dreams, and He will equip me sufficiently. More broadly, He will equip all of us sufficiently as a community of stewards. A community of Stewart Shipps, if I may say so.

Our desire is not that others might be relieved while you are hard pressed, but that there might be equality. At the present time your plenty will supply what they need, so that in turn their plenty will supply what you need. Then there will be equality, as it is written: "He who gathered much did not have too much, and he who gathered little did not have too little."

(2 Cor. 8:13-15)

That's God's promise of prosperity. Through the wisdom of our Sovereign God, we will have everything we need to serve and glorify Him wherever and however He desires and equips us to do so. Nothing more, nothing less. I want that. It's so equitable. So balanced. So logical. So perfect. So God.

Glen Smotherman
Peachtree Corners

Pleasant Word

To order additional copies of this title call:
1-877-421-READ (7323)
or please visit our web site at
www.pleasantwordbooks.com

If you enjoyed this quality custom published book,
drop by our web site for more books and information.

www.winepressgroup.com
"Your partner in custom publishing."